D0909461

Making the Difference for Teachers

This series is dedicated in loving memory
to my parents, Daisy Lea and Weldon F. Appelt.
Through their love and devotion for me, I learned to
believe in myself and what I might be able to achieve in life.

Making the Difference for Teachers

*The Field
Experience
in Actual
Practice*

Editor
Gloria Appelt Slick

CORWIN PRESS, INC.
A Sage Publications Company
Thousand Oaks, California

Copyright © 1995 by Corwin Press, Inc.

All rights reserved. No part of this book may be reproduced or utilized in any form or by any means, electronic or mechanical, including photocopying, recording, or by any information storage and retrieval system, without permission in writing from the publisher.

For information address:

Corwin Press, Inc.
A Sage Publications Company
2455 Teller Road
Thousand Oaks, California 91320

SAGE Publications Ltd.
6 Bonhill Street
London EC2A 4PU
United Kingdom

SAGE Publications India Pvt. Ltd.
M-32 Market
Greater Kailash I
New Delhi 110 048 India

Printed in the United States of America

Library of Congress Cataloging-in-Publication Data

Making the difference for teachers: the field experience in actual
  practice / edited by Gloria Appelt Slick
      p. cm.
    Includes bibliographical references and index.
    ISBN 0-8039-6210-X (alk. paper). — ISBN 0-8039-6211-8 (pbk.:
  alk. paper)
    1. Student teaching—United States.   2. Student teachers—
  Supervision of—United States.   I. Slick, Gloria Appelt.
  LB2157.U5M25   1995
  370'.7'330973—dc20   95-6675

This book is printed on acid-free paper.

95 96 97 98 99 10 9 8 7 6 5 4 3 2 1

Corwin Project Editor: Susan McElroy

Contents

Foreword

Student teaching has long been considered the capstone of the teacher education program, and early field experiences have recently become a vital part of preparing teachers. Most teacher educators believe that field experiences should be integrated into the preparation of future teachers.

Because of this emphasis on field experiences, the position of director of field experiences has become even more important in teacher education. Where can field directors receive the information necessary to carry out the many and varied duties of the position? They tend to ask other field directors' advice. One of the most popular opportunities for field directors to share ideas is through membership in the National Field Directors' Forum, an affiliate with the Association of Teacher Educators.

The tenure of a field director is relatively short. The average tenure is between 3 and 5 years. Because of the turnover of field directors, there always seem to be new field directors literally craving information that will help them perform their duties.

Field directors recognize the need for some books that contain the information that both experienced and new field directors could use as a reference. A series of four books dealing with all aspects of field experiences, edited by Dr. Gloria Appelt Slick, fulfills the need. Directors around the nation welcome this series and I am proud to endorse this effort.

ELDEN R. BARRETT, PH.D.
FORMER PRESIDENT, NATIONAL FIELD DIRECTORS' FORUM

Foreword

Dear Educator:

As you read the material presented in this four-book series dealing with field experiences in teacher preparation programs, I hope you will bear in mind that this unique project is being brought to you from an institution whose history is rich in and founded upon teacher education. It has been through the leadership and dedication of such educators as Dr. Gloria Appelt Slick, editor of this series, that The University of Southern Mississippi, which was founded as Mississippi's normal school in 1910, continues to take a leadership role in the professional training of teachers.

I am proud to share with you this most recent endeavor of Dr. Slick, which focuses on the significance of field experiences in teacher preparation. Recent research by the Holmes Group, John Goodlad, and such accrediting agencies as the National Council for the Accreditation of Teacher Education has underscored the importance of the field experiences component of teacher education programs. This series of four books provides a review of state-of-the-art programs and practices in field experiences. The contributing authors represent prestigious teacher preparation programs from around the country. The information presented herein is solidly grounded in both research and practice. One of the main purposes of the four books is to provide practical guidelines for application of effective programs and practices in field experiences.

This is not the first time Dr. Slick has produced a national project that emphasizes field experiences. In 1993, through a national teleconference under the auspices of the Satellite Educational Resources Consortium, four interactive distance learning programs were broadcast to more than 200 sites nationally for the purpose of assisting student teachers, during their student teaching experiences, with their transition from university students to classroom teachers. From that series and the research involved to produce it evolved the current books, whose purpose reaches beyond student teachers and encompasses all persons, processes, and institutions affected by the field experiences component of teacher education. In both cases, Dr. Slick's overall goal has been to provide assistance and direction for all those involved in field experiences so that students of teacher education will be better prepared to meet the challenges of teaching the children of today and tomorrow.

Teacher education will always remain a major focus at The University of Southern Mississippi. We are committed to excellence in our teacher preparation programs and strive to develop the best of each of our students' abilities and expertise as future teachers. It is through such efforts as Dr. Slick's that we strive to meet that commitment.

Best wishes,

AUBREY K. LUCAS
PRESIDENT, THE UNIVERSITY OF SOUTHERN MISSISSIPPI

Preface

As a result of the Holmes Report, "A Nation at Risk," and other research, the wheels have been set in motion for a reflective and systemic change in the education profession. Both public schools and institutions of higher learning have had the national, public spotlight on the quality of their educational outcomes and teacher preparation programs, respectively. Institutions of higher learning have adjusted their content and pedagogical requirements in their teacher education programs to try to meet the challenges of children who are products of the information age. Public schools have updated curricular offerings and made concerted efforts to tackle the innumerable problems relative to providing students and faculties with safe environments in which to teach and learn. Research by such educational leaders as Goodlad, Berliner, and Boyer emphasizes that the teachers of the future will need to participate early and continuously during their teacher preparation programs in the public school arena where they will eventually be employed. Nationwide, school districts and universities are forming collaborations that not only provide insight into the culture of the teaching profession for the novice teacher but also offer opportunities for veteran teachers to retool their skills as well as share their expertise with upcoming generations of new teachers. This bridge between the universities and the public schools, whether in the form of a professional development school, lab school, or local public school campus, provides, in essence, the pathway from student to teacher.

The program planning and management required to provide students in teacher preparation programs the opportunity to successfully cross the bridge from student to teacher are very complex. The bulk of the responsibility for providing students this successful crossing relies upon the collaborative success of teacher preparation programs and offices of educational field experiences. The director of the field experiences programs plays a principal role in managing the various persons and systems involved in the transitional passage of students to beginning teachers. It has been well documented by research that field experiences are the pivotal turning points in students' preparation for becoming teachers. During those experiences theory meets practice, and students discover whether they can teach or even want to teach. To date, for all persons and entities involved in this process, there is very little, if any, material available to assist in providing the best possible experiences for students aspiring to become exemplary teachers. The goal of this series of books is to provide field directors the information and practical guidance necessary to design and implement a successful field experience program that will provide individuals in teacher preparation programs a smooth transition from student to teacher.

Because the focus of these books is to provide information and practical guidance to all persons involved with field experiences in teacher preparation programs, it became a foregone conclusion that those persons contributing to this book should either be currently or have been recently affiliated with field experience programs. Most of the authors have actually been field experience directors, with the exception of those in specialty areas such as law and public school administration. In order for the book to be representative of a national view of the issues related to field experiences, much time and effort went into selecting persons representing a variety of types of institutions as well as geographic locations around the country. Attention has been given to the size of the teacher preparation programs offered at the various institutions that are represented in the books, with the intent to provide as many relevant views about field experience programs as possible in order to benefit cohorts everywhere. Institutions represented from the southeast include the states of Alabama,

Louisiana, Mississippi, Florida, and North Carolina; the northeast
includes the states of New Jersey, New York, Pennsylvania, and
Delaware; the midwestern states include Ohio, Kentucky, Illinois,
Michigan, Iowa, Indiana, and Minnesota; the central states include Oklahoma and Texas; and the western states include Colorado, Arizona, Utah, and California.

Organization of the Books

In order to provide information and practical guidance for all
the issues related to field experience programs, there are four
books, each with a specific purpose. Book I, *The Field Experience:
Creating Successful Programs for New Teachers*, provides information
about the development and organization of field experience programs. It presents state-of-the-art field experience programs and
explains what kinds of experiences should be provided to students.
Other issues in Book I include the dilemma of the department
chair who must provide a program that creates a balance between
theory and practica, the dean's perspective of the significance of
field experiences in teacher training, and the evaluation processes
needed for field experiences programs. Book II, *Preparing New
Teachers: Operating Successful Field Experience Programs*, presents
practical ideas concerning the operation and function of the field
experiences office and takes into account state department requirements relative to certification that also have an impact on
field experience programs. Such issues as placement procedures
as well as displacement procedures and the legal ramifications of
both are discussed. The multifaceted responsibilities of the field
director are presented, which brings to light the public relations
that the director must handle, not only with the public schools but
also across the various colleges and departments at a university/
college. In addition, the purposes of field experiences handbooks
are explained. Book III, *Making the Difference for Teachers: The Field
Experience in Actual Practice*, addresses the needs and responsibilities of the persons involved in a typical field experience
paradigm—the university student, public school personnel, and
university personnel. Key issues such as effective communication

and classroom management skills, effective mentoring, and adequate training of cooperating teachers are presented. Field experiences are explained from the student teacher's perspective, and the process of the student's assimilation of the culture of teaching is addressed. A major issue of concern is the preparation of cooperating teachers for the responsibility of supervising students. This is also dealt with in Book III. In addition, suggestions are made for ways to express appreciation to those who work so diligently supervising student teachers and other practicum students. Each of these issues has an impact on the university students' success during field experiences, and each topic is delivered in practical and applicable terms. Book IV, *Emerging Trends in Teacher Preparation: The Future of Field Experiences,* addresses areas of special interest affecting field experiences: (a) the promotion of reflective practices throughout all field experiences in teacher preparation programs; (b) the multicultural classroom environments education students will have to face; (c) the effective utilization of technology in field experience programs; (d) the awareness of legal ramifications of policies, or the lack of them, in field experience programs; (e) the development of leadership potential in pre-service teachers; (f) the support for the first year on the job; and (g) the special opportunities for student teaching field experiences abroad. A new look at the psychology of supervision is also presented along with a view of how the past can help us shape the future in field experiences. At the end of each book, there is a chapter titled "Bits and Pieces" that presents other issues that are critical to the overall success of field experience programs. Key points mentioned in each book are synthesized and analyzed. The information is presented in a somewhat encapsulated view along with additional points that may need mentioning.

The composite focus of all four books of the series is to provide the information and operational examples to assist others in offering strong, challenging, and viable field experiences programs throughout the country. The reader will find that each topic addressed in the books will place an emphasis on the practical application of the ideas and information presented. The series of books will provide readers not only with "food for thought" but also "food for action."

Acknowledgments

A massive project like this is only possible because of many wonderful people contributing their expertise, time, and energy into making it happen. From all over the country friends and colleagues worked diligently to contribute a special piece to one of the books. My sincere appreciation to my authors who patiently worked with me to complete this series.

Thanks also go to my office staff, Tina Holmes and Diane Ross, and university supervisors, Drs. Donna Garvey, Tammie Brown, Betsy Ward, and Ed Lundin, who kept the office running smoothly while I labored over "the books," as they came to be known in the office. Our office teamwork and philosophy of operation paid off during this project. Thanks go to my graduate assistants, Leslie Peebles and Amy Palughi, whose hard work during the initial stages of this project launched us with a good beginning. Most especially thanks go to Mrs. Lauree Mills Mooney, whose organizational and computer skills made it possible for the project to be pulled together in a timely manner. Mrs. Mooney's resourcefulness in overcoming obstacles and dedication toward completing the project were invaluable. In the final stages of proofing and indexing all the books, I want to thank Ms. Holly Henderson for her timely and critical assistance.

Thanks to special friends who encouraged me throughout the project: Dr. Margaret Smith, Dr. Kenneth Burrett, Dr. Chuck Jaquith, and Dr. Sandra Gupton.

The timely production and final completion of all four books could not have occurred without the kind and caring encouragement and guidance of the Corwin Press staff. My sincere thanks go to Alice Foster, Marlene Head, Wendy Appleby, Susan McElroy, and Lin Schonberger for their understanding and patience throughout this project.

A special thanks to my husband, Sam Slick, for his constant encouragement and support. Also, special thanks to my children, Andrew and Samantha, who patiently tiptoed around the house so Mom could think and compose in order to finish "the books."

About the Contributors

Sharon Brennan is an assistant professor and the director of Field Experiences and School Collaboration in Education at the University of Kentucky. Her research interests include teacher effectiveness and teacher evaluation, and she recently edited a handbook designed to train evaluation team members for the Kentucky Teacher Internship Program. Among other endeavors, she teaches a graduate course in clinical supervision, supervises student teachers, and teaches an undergraduate course on community service in public schools, which requires students to participate in an after-school tutoring program.

Kenneth Burrett is a professor in the school of education at Duquesne University and an associate in the center for character education, civic responsibility, and teaching. He also serves as a charter faculty member for Duquesne University's Interdisciplinary Doctoral Program for Education Leaders. A former elementary and secondary teacher and high school department chair, he has served as director of student teaching and associate dean at Duquesne. He received his bachelor of arts and master of science degrees from Canisius College and his Ed.D. from the State University of New York at Buffalo. He is active in Phi Delta Kappa, the Pennsylvania Association of Colleges and Teacher Educators (PAC-TE), and the Association for Teacher Educators (ATE). He was named Teacher Educator of the Year in 1989 by the Pennsylvania Unit of ATE. He serves on the board of Conservation Consultants, a nonprofit environmental organization; is past president of Western Pennsylvania Council for the Social Sciences; and serves on the board of PAC-TE and various committees of ATE. He has also secured numerous grants for in-servicing veteran science teachers and encouraging career change individuals to enter teaching. This past year he coauthored a book chapter and *Phi Delta Kappa Fastback*, both concerned with integrated character education. He has also delivered numerous papers in the area of leadership theory and program design.

Lesley Peebles Fairley is a teacher at Ocean Springs Junior High School in Ocean Springs, Mississippi. She earned a bachelor of science degree as well as a master's degree in elementary education from The University of Southern Mississippi in Hattiesburg. Currently in her second year of teaching, she is actively involved in the transition Ocean Springs Junior High is making to become a middle school and is also a part-time gymnastics instructor. She plans to continue her education by beginning work on her doctorate in the summer of 1995. With a passion for children's literature and art, she will also continue to create and illustrate her own children's book.

Marvin A. Henry is a professor of education at Indiana State University, where his area of specialization is field experiences. He has supervised more than 2,000 student teachers during his career. His book, *Supervising Student Teachers the Professional Way*, now in its fourth edition, is used as a reference for cooperating teachers and a standard textbook for courses in the supervision of student teaching. He frequently serves as a consultant for groups concerned with student teaching and field experiences. In 1986 he developed a model intern program, which received the Distinguished Program in Teacher Education Award from the Association of Teacher Educators. An active professional leader, he is a former president and also Distinguished Member of the Association of Teacher Educators.

Robert E. Knaub is coordinator of field experiences at Oklahoma State University. He has been directly involved with student teaching programs during his 28-year career. As an assistant principal, and later as a principal, he was directly involved with the orientation, assigning, and development of student teachers in his building. He was also directly involved in a project that identified the most important characteristics that pre-student teachers need in order to be successful in teaching. Later, this model was used nationally to identify potential teachers. As a successful high school and middle-level teacher, he has mentored many student teachers.

Sharon O'Bryan is education consultant, Division of Performance-Based Accreditation, Center for School Assessment, Research, and Information Technology, Indiana Department of Education. She has been director of student teaching at Indiana University, Education Department chair at William Woods University, and a professor in the Department of Curriculum and Instruction at Southwest Texas State University. She has been active in the field of teacher induction as a researcher, presenter, and trainer. In the 1987-1988 school year she was the principal investigator of a pilot induction project and has presented findings from this study at national, state, and regional teacher education conferences. In 1990 she was part of a grant writing team awarded a large grant for designing mentor training programs. She also served on the training team that developed and implemented the training program for more than 300 mentor teachers in the Houston ISD mentor teacher program during the 1988-1989 school year, and she has trained mentor teachers from more than 15 Central Texas school districts. Because of her expertise in teacher induction, she was asked to serve as a reviewer for the recent book, *Mentoring: Developing Successful New Teachers*, produced by the Association of Teacher Educators' Commission on The Role and Preparation of Mentor Teachers. In 1990 Dr. O'Bryan was named as one of the nation's 70 Outstanding Teacher Educators by the Association of Teacher Educators.

William Watson Purkey is professor of Counselor Education at the University of North Carolina at Greensboro and co-founder of the International Alliance for Invitational Education. His professional experience includes teaching as a public school teacher, as an explosive ordinance disposal specialist in the United States Air Force, and as a university professor. He has been awarded the University of Florida Student Award for Instructor Excellence, The Standard Oil Foundation Good Teaching Award, and the Outstanding Teacher Award by Omicron Delta Kappa National Leadership Honor Society. He is also the recipient of the Distinguished Alumnus Award, given by the School of Education, University of Virginia; the John McGovern Award, presented by the American School Health Association; and the Professional Development Award, presented by the American Counseling Association. In 1991 he received the University of North Carolina at Greensboro Alumni Teaching Excellence Award. An active writer, lecturer, and researcher, he has authored or coauthored more than 80 professional articles and eight books, including *Self-Concept and School Achievement* and *Inviting School Success*, now in its second edition. Dr. Purkey's interest is in inviting people to realize their potential; his latest coauthored book is *The Inviting School Treasury*.

Margaret H. Shaw-Baker is an assistant professor of education and Field Experiences Coordinator of Clinical Experiences for the Department of Curriculum and Instruction at Illinois State University (ISU). She has worked with student teachers since 1979, at both the ISU Peoria and McLean County Teacher Education Centers. She served as director of the McLean County Teacher Education Center for 10 years. She also teaches classes for cooperating teachers affiliated with ISU's clinical field experiences.

Gloria Appelt Slick, a native of Houston, Texas, completed her doctoral work at the University of Houston in 1979. Her professional career in public school education has included classroom teaching, supervision, the principalship, and assistant superintendency for curriculum. In her current position as a faculty member of the Department of Curriculum and Instruction and as Director of Educational Field Experiences at The University of Southern Mississippi in Hattiesburg, Mississippi, her past public school experiences have provided her with significant insight into the circumstances and needs of public schools for well-trained beginning teachers. During her tenure as Director of Field Experiences, Dr. Slick has produced, in conjunction with Mississippi Educational Television, the first interactive distance learning program to deal with the subject of field experiences, titled "From Student to Teacher." These four programs were aired nationally in March 1993 and received the Mississippi Public Education Forum Award for Excellence that same year. Dr. Slick is currently president of the National Field Directors' Forum, affiliated with the Association of Teacher Educators. She also serves on the editorial board of *The Teacher Educator*. Her current research interests center on teacher preparation programs and, in particular, the interface of field experiences with those programs. Technological integration into the field experience programs and field experiences abroad are also high on her list of research and programmatic implementation.

Sandra Weiser is an assistant dean of the College of Education at the University of Northern Colorado. She is a native of Michigan, where she did her undergraduate at Grand Valley State University and her graduate work at Michigan State University. Her public school background includes 7 years of classroom teaching and administrative experience as a curriculum coordinator and an assistant superintendent. She taught reading and study skills at the University of Wisconsin, and she has taught education methods and reading courses and served as a supervisor of student teachers at the University of Northern Colorado. She has held her current position for the past 7 years and is responsible for the Teacher Education Center at UNC.

Patricia T. Whitfield is currently dean of the Division of Education at Heritage College in Toppenish, Washington. She has been an elementary teacher, education consultant, college/university faculty member, program chair, director of field experiences, assistant dean, and dean. She considers herself first and foremost a teacher educator. Although her interests are diverse, she is especially committed to quality field-based teacher education, faculty development, and educational equity.

Introduction

GLORIA APPELT SLICK

Educational philosophies that form the foundation for field experience programs and the office management operation of a field experience program are all vital to the success of field experience. It is, however, the people who are implementing the programs and living them on a day-to-day basis who really make the difference. *Making the Difference for Teachers: The Field Experience in Actual Practice* explores the internal workings of the relationships and events that have an impact on all the persons involved during field experiences. Several chapters deal with the unique roles and responsibilities that professionals from both the university and the public schools must assume. For a field experience program to be successful, it is critical that the persons engaged in it be well trained to meet the challenges they face in competently fulfilling their responsibilities. It is proposed that:

> [T]he primary task of supervisors of instruction is to create conditions in which teachers can become vigorous investigators of the thinking and action that motivate their teaching. Thus, cooperating teachers, college/university

supervisors of student teachers and supervisors of inservice teachers must prompt clients to consider how and
why they are doing what they are doing. (Cruickshank &
Kennedy, 1977, p. 51)

The relationships among the student teacher, cooperating
teacher, and university supervisor are key to the success of the
field experience. Each must clearly understand his or her responsibilities as well as those of the others. One of the best ways to
provide this understanding is through effective communication.
Effective communication skills are just one set of skills needed by
all three persons in order for a quality field experience to occur.
There is a definite need for cooperating teachers and university
supervisors to participate in training opportunities that will teach
them to be effective mentors, instructional planners, and evaluators, as well as effective communicators. The dual role of support
agent and evaluator, which both the cooperating teacher and the
university supervisor play, is not an easy one. On one hand, they
are nurturing the growth of a neophyte teacher; on the other, they
are evaluating the progress and issuing the final grade. A clear
understanding of both roles and their responsibilities is a necessity if a cooperating teacher and university supervisor are going
to be effective.

The student teachers are treading in unfamiliar territory during the student teaching experience. Full of pedagogical ideals
and, in most cases, unbridled enthusiasm for getting into the
classroom (frequently referred to as the "real world"), they launch
into their first, full-time instructional experience with great anticipation and anxiety. Once on site, they begin an acculturation
process into the profession that is both common to all instructional
campuses and specific to the one to which they have been assigned. It means becoming a part of a faculty, but not really. It
means learning all about the operational functions of the school
they are in, as well as the district to which they have been assigned. In other words, they begin the process of assimilating the
culture of teaching. One of the most difficult and perplexing issues
they must deal with is becoming a manager/disciplinarian in
someone else's classroom. The issue of classroom management

becomes a looming problem because, as most research will corroborate, student teachers do not typically feel prepared to handle classroom management. In many cases, the student teacher only gets to parrot what is being done by the cooperating teacher. Consequently, the preservice teacher still doesn't learn how he or she will manage his or her own classroom.

Included in this book is the student teacher's perspective of field experiences. Views of administrators concerning the purposes of field experiences on their campuses are also presented. Rewards for cooperating teachers' special efforts to help preservice teachers are also discussed. Ideas and proven methods for saying "thank you" are described.

Finally, this book explores the need to prepare teachers to teach in invitational schools. These schools strive to facilitate learning in a positive, caring, and respectful environment. Learning is valued and is sought with energetic enthusiasm. The classroom environment of the future will also provide acceptance and appreciation for all students and the diversity they bring to the classroom.

Keeping the public schools alive and well in the next century will be no small task. As we move toward the next century our profession is experiencing massive reform and systemic change. The search is for an educational model that will provide young people with the kind of education they will need to function in a high-tech society. Schools cannot continue to be steeped in a long historical heritage of tradition and unwavering change. The advent of the information age is catapulting society out of the reach of traditional schools. Schools must meet the challenge or face the reality that instructional technology will put the classroom in the home. People need to share ideas, to experiment and manipulate concepts both mentally and physically. We also need to learn to cooperatively function as law-abiding citizens. Public schools must provide these learning opportunities. Schools and universities must work cooperatively together to meet the challenge of educating tomorrow's youths. Therefore, together they must design and implement teacher preparation programs that provide society with savvy educators who can challenge the information age child to meet his or her potential.

Reference

Cruickshank, D., & Kennedy, J. (1977). The role of significant others during the student teaching experience. *Journal of Teacher Education, 28*(5), 51-55.

Preparing Invitational Teachers for Next-Century Schools

WILLIAM WATSON PURKEY

Perhaps never before in American history have beginning teachers faced such challenges. More and more young teachers are entering urban neighborhoods where violence is a way of life, where students lack trust in adults, and where top-down, authoritarian leadership is a chronic problem.

Young teachers are hit with mounds of paperwork and countless reports to be completed. They face a host of nonteaching responsibilities, including locker checks, monthly registers, floating schedules, hall monitoring, bus duty, drug and weapon checks, and challenges that traditional teacher education training programs never cover.

Faced with what appears to be a powerfully "disinviting" situation, it is tempting for the young teacher to join the ranks of disillusioned teachers, who not only have given up on themselves as teachers but also work to discourage the beginning teacher. The

1

purpose of this chapter is to suggest a process whereby professors in schools of education can work to revitalize and transform the training of young teachers so that they can withstand the incredible pressure of teaching in contemporary schools. The process is called "invitational teaching" (Purkey & Novak, 1984, 1995; Purkey & Stanley, 1991).

Invitational Teaching

Invitational teaching is centered on four propositions that give it purpose and direction. The four are *trust, respect, optimism,* and *intentionality.*

Trust: The teaching-learning process should be a cooperative, collaborative activity in which process is as important as product. A basic ingredient of invitational teaching is a recognition of the interdependence of human beings. Attempting to teach students without involving them in the process is a lost cause. Even if the effort to get students to do what is wanted without their cooperation is successful, the energy expended by the teacher is usually disproportionate to what is accomplished.

Respect: People are able, valuable, and capable of being responsible, and they should be treated accordingly. An indispensable element in any classroom is shared responsibility based on mutual respect. In tough schools, to "diss" a student (to show disrespect) is a serious affront that can trigger violence. Respect is manifested in the caring and appropriate behaviors exhibited by the teacher.

Optimism: People possess untapped potential in all areas of human endeavor. The uniqueness of human beings is that no clear limits to potential have been discovered. Invitational teaching could not be seriously considered if optimism regarding human potential did not exist.

Intentionality: Human potential can best be realized by places, policies, processes, and programs specifically designed to invite develop-

ment and by teachers who are intentionally inviting with themselves and others, personally and professionally. Intentionality is the structure that gives meaning to experience. It enables invitational teachers to create and maintain consistently caring and appropriate classrooms characterized by purpose and direction.

The four essential propositions of invitational teaching—trust, respect, optimism, and intentionality—offer a consistent *stance* through which teachers can create and maintain an optimally inviting classroom environment. Though there are other elements that contribute to invitational teaching, these four assumptions are key ingredients.

To understand invitational teaching it is vital to give primary attention to the teacher's person. Invitational teaching has a much wider focus of application than is typically considered in teacher education programs. It is deliberately aimed at broader goals than students and their achievement alone. It is geared to the total development of all who interact within the school. It is concerned with more than grades, attendance, and even perceptions of self. Invitational teaching is concerned with the skills of becoming.

Attention to the person in the process must be more than that presented in traditional courses in educational psychology and human development. These courses tend to place heavy emphasis on research that may have little to do with real people working with real students in real classrooms. Any psychology or human development course that seeks to be of benefit to young teachers must encompass the total personalities and behaviors of teachers and students in constant interaction. It is important that they focus on characteristics that are more important than knowledge of subject matter or proficiency in skills, methods, and techniques.

It is useful to pause here and contemplate the complexity of invitational teaching. Many teachers think they already understand the concept of "inviting." They see it as simply doing nice things—sharing a smile, giving a hug, saying something nice, or buying a gift, but invitational teaching is far more than giving "warm fuzzies," sharing "strokes," forming "hug stations," or walking around with IALAC ("*I* Am Lovable *A*nd Capable) newsprint. Although these may be worthwhile activities when used

caringly and appropriately, they are only manifestations of a theoretical stance one takes as a teacher. This stance determines the
level of functioning and provides a way to monitor one's behavior,
both personally and professionally.

Levels of Functioning

There are many ways to categorize teacher behavior. Invitational teaching identifies four categories: (a) intentionally disinviting, (b) unintentionally disinviting, (c) unintentionally inviting,
and (d) intentionally inviting. When teachers reach and are consistently functioning at the fourth level, then the *plus factor* comes
into play. It will be helpful to consider these levels.

Intentionally Disinviting

The most negative and toxic level of human functioning involves those actions, policies, programs, places, and processes
that are deliberately designed to demean, dissuade, discourage,
defeat, and destroy. A classic example of intentionally disinviting
behavior in action may be seen in the play *Amadeus*. It is Salieri
who is intentionally disinviting—with great destructive skill—to
Mozart.

In educational settings, intentionally disinviting functioning
might be seen in a teacher who is purposely insulting, a school
policy that is intentionally discriminatory, a program that purposely demeans students, or an environment intentionally left
unpleasant and unattractive.

An illustration of intentionally disinviting functioning was
provided by a high school teacher. After attending a workshop on
invitational teaching, this teacher sent a note to the principal,
pointing out that the girls' bathroom needed soap, paper towels,
and tissue. Her note was returned to her mailbox at the end of the
day, with this remark written across the bottom (unsigned): "What
do you think this place is—the Hilton?" With such an intentionally
disinviting stance, is it any wonder that teachers in this particular
school are so apathetic, or students so unruly?

Unintentionally Disinviting

Teachers who are intentionally disinviting are few when compared to those who are unintentionally disinviting. The great majority of disinviting forces that exist in and around schools are the result of a lack of stance. Because there is no philosophy of trust, respect, optimism, and intentionality, policies are established, programs are designed, places are arranged, processes evolve, and teachers behave in ways that are clearly disinviting although such was not the intent.

Teachers who function at the unintentionally disinviting level are often viewed as uncaring, chauvinistic, condescending, patronizing, sexist, racist, dictatorial, or just plain thoughtless. They do not intend to be hurtful or harmful, but because they lack consistency in direction and purpose, they act in unintentionally disinviting ways. Examples of unintentionally disinviting forces at work can be seen in almost any school: the sign that reads "No One Allowed In School Before 8:15 a.m." (although the temperature is below zero), the policy of reserving the best parking space for the principal, the tendency to answer the office phone with a curt "Jackson Junior," or teachers who consistently kick students "in the but" ("This is a good paper, Mary, but . . . "). Teachers who function at the unintentionally disinviting level do not intend to be disinviting, but the damage is done. Like being run over by a truck, intended or not, the victim is still dead.

Unintentionally Inviting

Teachers who usually function at the unintentionally inviting level have stumbled serendipitously into ways of functioning that are often effective. However, they encounter difficulty when asked to explain *why* they are successful. They can describe in loving detail *what* they do, but not *why*.

An illustration of unintentionally inviting functioning might be seen in "natural born" teachers. They may be successful in teaching because they exhibit many of the trusting, respecting, and optimistic qualities associated with invitational teaching. However, because they lack the fourth critical element, intentionality, they lack consistency and dependability in the actions they exhibit, the policies and programs they establish, and the places and processes they create and maintain.

Young teachers often function at the unintentionally inviting level. Though they are likable, entertaining, enthusiastic, and committed, they lack intentionality regarding why they are doing what they do. These teachers are somewhat akin to the early barnstorming airplane pilots. Pioneer pilots did not know exactly why their planes flew, what caused weather patterns, or much about navigational systems. As long as they stayed close to the ground, they followed a railway track, and the weather was clear, they were able to function. When the weather turned bad or night fell, they became disoriented and lost. In difficult situations, those who function at the unintentionally inviting level lack dependability in behavior and consistency in direction.

The basic weakness in functioning at the unintentionally inviting level is the inability to identify the reasons for success or failure. Most teachers know whether something is working or not, but when it stops working, they are puzzled about how to start it up again. Those who function at the unintentionally inviting level lack a consistent stance—a dependable position from which to operate.

Intentionally Inviting

When teachers function at the intentionally inviting level, they seek to consistently exhibit the assumptions of invitational teaching. A beautiful example of intentionality in action is presented by Mizer (1964), who described how schools can function to turn a child "into a zero." Mizer illustrated the tragedy of one such child, then concluded her article with these words:

> I look up and down the rows carefully each September at the unfamiliar faces. I look for veiled eyes or bodies scrunched into a seat in an alien world. "Look, Kids," I say silently, "I may not do anything else for you this year, but not one of you is going to come out of here a nobody. I'll

work or fight to the bitter end doing battle with society and the school board, but I won't have one of you coming out of here thinking of himself as a zero." (p. 10)

Intentionality can be a tremendous asset for teachers, for it is a constant reminder of what is truly important in education. Those who accept the assumptions of invitational teaching not only strive to be intentionally inviting but, once there, continue to grow and develop, to reach for the plus factor.

The Plus Factor

When people watch the accomplished musician, the headline comedian, the world-class athlete, or the master teacher, what he or she does seems simple. It is only when people try to do it themselves that they realize that true art requires painstaking care, discipline, and deliberate planning.

At its best, invitational teaching becomes "invisible" because it becomes a means of addressing humanity. To borrow the words of Chuang-tse, an ancient Chinese philosopher: "It flows like water, reflects like a mirror, and responds like an echo." When the teacher reaches this special plateau, what he or she does appears effortless. Football teams call it "momentum," comedians call it "feeling the center," world-class athletes call it "finding the zone," and fighter pilots call it "rhythm." In invitational teaching it is called the plus factor. A good example of this factor in action was provided by Ginger Rogers, the famous actress and dancer. When describing dancing with Fred Astaire, she said, "It's a lot of hard work, that I do know." Someone responded, "But it doesn't look it, Ginger." Ginger replied, "That's why it's magic."

Teachers who function at the highest levels of inviting become so fluent that the carefully honed skills and techniques they employ are invisible to the untrained eye. They function with such talented assurance that the tremendous effort involved does not call attention to itself. At its best, invitational teaching requires implicit, rather than explicit, expression.

Dimensions of Inviting

The goal of invitational teaching is to encourage teachers to enrich their lives in each of four basic dimensions: (a) being personally inviting with oneself, (b) being personally inviting with others, (c) being professionally inviting with oneself, and (d) being professionally inviting with others. Like pistons in a finely tuned engine, the four dimensions work together to give power to the whole movement. Though there are times when one of the four dimensions may demand special attention, the overall goal is to seek balance and harmony between personal and professional functioning.

Being Personally Inviting With Oneself. To be a beneficial presence in the lives of students, it is essential that teachers first invite themselves. This means that they view themselves as able, valuable, and responsible, and are open to experience. Educators who adopt invitational teaching seek to reinvent and respirit themselves personally.

Being personally inviting with oneself takes an endless variety of forms. It means caring for one's mental health and making appropriate choices in life. By taking up a new hobby, relaxing with a good book, exercising regularly, learning to laugh more, visiting friends, getting sufficient sleep, growing a garden, or managing time wisely, teachers can rejuvenate their own well-being.

Being Personally Inviting With Others. Being inviting requires that the feelings, wishes, and aspirations of others be taken into account. Without this, invitational teaching could not exist. In practical terms, this means that the social committee might be the most vital committee in any school.

Specific ways to be personally inviting with others are simple but often overlooked. Getting to know colleagues on a social basis, sending friendly notes, forming a carpool, remembering birthdays, enjoying a faculty party, practicing politeness, and celebrating successes are all examples of invitational teaching in action.

Being Professionally Inviting With Oneself. Being professionally inviting with oneself can take a variety of forms, but it begins with ethical awareness and a clear perception of situations and oneself. In practical terms, being professionally inviting with oneself means trying a new teaching method, seeking certification, learning new skills, returning to graduate school, enrolling in workshops, attending conferences, reading journals, writing for publication, and making presentations at conferences.

Invitational teaching requires that educators not "rust" on their laurels. Keeping alive professionally is particularly important for educators because of the rapidly expanding knowledge base regarding teaching and learning. Invitational teaching not only involves encounters with students in caring and appropriate ways but also involves the teacher's relationship with the content of what is being taught. Perhaps never before in North American education have knowledge, techniques, and methods been so bountiful. Canoes must be paddled harder than ever just to keep up with the quickening river of knowledge.

Being Professionally Inviting With Others. The final dimension of invitational teaching is being professionally inviting with others. This involves such qualities as treating people not as labels or groups, but as individuals. It also requires honesty and the ability to accept the less-than-perfect behavior of human beings.

In everyday practice, being professionally inviting with others requires careful attention to the policies that are introduced, the programs established, the places created, the processes manifested, and the behaviors exhibited. Among the countless ways that teachers can be professionally inviting with others are to have high aspirations, fight sexism and racism in any form, work cooperatively, behave ethically, provide professional feedback, and maintain an optimistic stance.

Professionals who combine the four dimensions of invitational teaching into a seamless whole are well on their way to mastering their profession. The successful teacher is one who balances the four dimensions to sustain energy and enthusiasm for teaching, learning, and living.

The first half of this chapter has presented invitational teaching as a guiding theory of practice based on trust, respect, optimism and intentionality. It highlighted levels of functioning and dimensions in personal and professional behavior. The second part of this chapter focuses on the qualities of inviting teachers that are similar to the characteristics of self-actualizing individuals.

The Characteristics of Self-Actualizing Individuals

Continuing research in counseling and psychotherapy has confirmed the existence of several characteristics of self-actualizing behavior that are included, either explicitly or implicitly, in virtually every major theory or approach to counseling or psychotherapy, though differing terminology has been used. Three of the basic conditions that have been identified are empathy, respect, and genuineness.

Empathy

Empathy is understanding of another person from that person's point of view. This internal frame of reference is achieved by putting oneself in the place of the other so that one sees, as closely as possible, as that person does (Patterson, 1985). Rogers's definition perhaps expresses it as well as any: "[A]n accurate, empathic understanding of the [other's] world as seen from the inside. To sense the [other's] private world as if it were your own, but without losing the 'as if' quality—this is empathy" (Rogers, 1961, p. 284). To teach a student, it is imperative that the teacher know something about that student from the student's point of view.

There are no synonyms for empathic understanding. Unlike other languages, English does not have two words to designate the two kinds of understanding or knowing: knowing about, and the knowing that is empathy. Both kinds of knowing can be taught in teacher education programs. Unfortunately, only one is taught in most colleges and universities.

Respect

The second condition is a deep respect for people, an unconditional acceptance of the other person as he or she is, without judgment or condemnation, criticism, ridicule, or depreciation. It is a respect that includes a warmth and liking for another as a person, with all his or her faults, deficiencies, and undesirable or unacceptable behavior. It is a deep interest and concern for the person and his or her development. Being respected by a teacher can be a powerful force in inviting positive self-respect in students (Purkey & Novak, 1984, 1995; Purkey & Stanley, 1991).

Genuineness

Genuineness is the congruence or integration of the teacher in the professional relationship. "It means that within the relationship he [or she] is freely and deeply himself [or herself], with his [or her] actual experience, accurately represented by his [or her] awareness of himself [or herself]" (Rogers, 1957, p. 95). The teacher is not thinking or feeling one thing and saying another. He or she is open, honest, and sincere, without a facade and without playing some stereotypical role.

The conditions of empathy, respect, and genuineness are not new and certainly not revolutionary. Yet their consistent application in interpersonal relations might well be revolutionary in teacher education programs. If one considers the totality of the facilitative conditions—ability to understand, like, and prize individuals; empathy; concern; acceptance; respect; warmth; sincerity; openness; authenticity—they add up to a concept that has long been recognized as basic to good human relationships. The Greeks had a word for it: *agape*. St. Paul called it *love*.

These characteristics—empathy, respect or nonpossessive warmth, and genuineness—manifested by teachers are the necessary conditions not only for affective learning but also for cognitive learning (Aspy, Roebuck, & Benoit, 1987; Carkhuff, 1987; Whitman, Spendlove, & Clark, 1986). They are the necessary conditions for self-initiated, meaningful, experiential learning, enabling the student to actualize his or her limitless potentialities.

The Focus of Teacher Education

It is the person within the teacher that is the most important factor in teaching and learning. It should therefore be apparent that teacher education should focus on the development of the person within the teacher. This requires primary attention to the feelings, attitudes, and beliefs of teachers, including all the attitudes, opinions, and beliefs the teachers hold to be true regarding their own personal existence: their self-concept.

That good teachers differ from poor teachers in their belief systems was discovered early by Combs and associates. In *Florida Studies in the Helping Professions* (Combs, Soper, Gooding, Benton, Dickman, & Usher, 1969), good teachers, compared to poor ones, perceived others as able rather than unable, as friendly rather than unfriendly, as worthy rather than undependable, and as helpful rather than hindering. These same studies also found that good teachers perceived themselves differently from poor teachers perceived themselves. Compared to poor teachers, good teachers perceived themselves as more adequate, trustworthy, and wanted, and they tended to identify more with other human beings.

What are the implications of these findings for teacher education programs? It is not the purpose of this chapter to deal with the total program of teacher education, but only that part that deals with the teacher's person: the conditions that facilitate the development and maintenance of self-actualizing individuals.

Some Specific Suggestions for Teacher Education

There are special pressures and particular forms of isolation that are brought about by being a teacher. The attention given to the development of academic knowledge and instructional skills must not overlook the person who is to teach and the student who is to learn. Society needs not only persons with cognitive abilities, who can read, write, and calculate—the three Rs—but also citizens who can relate to others—the fourth R—interpersonal relationships.

Teachers can be prepared for the interpersonal relationship aspect of education. The following are six practical suggestions important for the preparation of teachers for the 21st century. These suggestions are based on a person-centered approach to the educative process first described by Carl Rogers, A. W. Combs, C. H. Patterson, and others who gave primary emphasis in teacher preparation programs to the people in the process: the attitudinal qualities that exist in human relationships.

Focus on the Teacher Educators. Emphasis needs to be upon the conditions for facilitating the development of invitational teachers for next-century schools. These conditions are the same for the development of self-actualizing professors in teacher-education programs. If society wants teacher-educators who are capable of fostering self-actualization in their students, then these teachers of teachers must themselves be self-actualizing persons. They can become such persons by experiencing the conditions that are necessary for the development of self-actualizing persons. The manner in which the conditions operate is complex, but one important aspect of the nature of the influence is what is called modeling. One becomes like those with whom one associates or engages over time in close interpersonal relationships. Teachers are models for their students, and teacher educators are models for their students. Teacher educators who advocate invitational teaching for their students must practice what they preach. What educators do speaks louder than what they say.

Establish an Internal Frame of Reference. Traditional teacher education programs have focused on objective observation: reporting what is observed without personal bias or distortion. This emphasis on objectivity has often blinded student teachers to the feelings, attitudes, perceptions, goals, and purposes of the pupil: to see things from the pupil's side of the desk. Being able to place oneself in the shoes of students, particularly those students who are different from the teacher, helps to promote an appreciation of diversity and to discourage bigotry, racism, sexism, and cultural intolerance.

Laboratory experiences for student teachers and teacher interns should offer practice in taking the internal frame of reference in interaction with individuals. This training can begin with learning to recognize the existence of various levels of the conditions of empathy, respect, and genuineness. Role-playing is a valuable aspect of laboratory experience in developing these conditions. This, and actual supervised laboratory experiences, offers opportunities for the student to engage in self-exploration regarding his or her beliefs and attitudes, leading to better self-understanding and the possibility of positive change in one's self-concept. Such experiences should be accompanied by seminars in which students discuss their observations and experiences, and also their philosophy, beliefs, and attitudes toward themselves and others. These continuous integrative seminars will be considered later in this chapter.

Select Supervising Teachers Carefully. The classroom internship, which is one of the most important experiences in teacher education, can be one of its major problems. The practicing classroom teacher (the supervising or critic teacher) with whom the student does his or her internship and practice teaching is a critical influence on the teacher education student, becoming a model for the student. Yet, such teachers are typically chosen on the recommendation of a principal or superintendent, whose concept of a "good" teacher may be essentially one who maintains good discipline and control, and not one who is student centered.

There is much that can be done to improve the classroom internship and its supervision. A good model can be found in the teaching of counseling students, where the student is given the opportunity to engage, under supervision, in real counseling with real clients, and where he or she has real responsibility for the counseling situation. This experience requires the student to develop a theory of counseling and a system of principles that can be applied to a great variety of specific situations. The supervisor becomes the primary facilitator for the student's development. In teacher education, the supervisor also becomes the facilitator of the student teacher's personal and professional development.

Use Group Processes Frequently. The essence of successful professional work with people is the effective use of the self as instrument. Teacher education should focus on the development of the teacher as a person: a person who can offer the necessary conditions of learning and self-actualization to others. Thus, the general atmosphere of the teacher education program, including policies, places, and processes, contributes to the development of an adequate and helping self.

Individual counseling can and does help, though to make it available to every student or to require it of all students would be prohibitive. It should certainly be available for those who need and want it. Perhaps the most effective method for developing invitational teachers who can facilitate the personal development of their students is the experience provided by group counseling.

Group counseling is a vital component in developing appreciation for cultural and social diversity, which is, or should be, an essential objective of teacher education programs. As Cazden and Mehan (1989) pointed out, "teacher education can help beginning teachers learn how to learn experientially about students and their families and encourage them to reflect on their own cultural background rather than unthinkingly live it as an unexamined norm" (p. 55). It is ineffective to provide information about cultural and social differences without providing group activities through which students can discover the personal meanings of this information.

Group experiences can be a great help in assisting teachers to be in touch with their own feelings when working with students, provided these experiences are conducted by qualified counselors. Recent approaches, such as student peer coaching, peer tutoring, and peer helping, can best be directed by teachers who are themselves prepared in the nature of groups and group processes.

Conduct Continuous, Integrative Seminars. Although group processes are concerned with personal development and interpersonal relationships, students also benefit from the opportunity to participate in continuous, integrative professional seminars in which they can, with the instructor and with one another, consider, evaluate, and integrate their total experience in teacher education, including instructional content, laboratory experiences, and other activities. This should also include their personal and professional development in terms of ideas, beliefs, attitudes, and their philosophy of education. This seminar should be a continuing one from the very beginning of their teacher program to its end, including the internship teaching experience. As Cohen (1991), Kagan (1992), Louden (1991), and others have pointed out, the practice of teaching is anchored in the belief system and personality of the teacher.

Continuing seminars are also valuable for teachers-to-be to examine who they are and how they see their career choice. Too often, young adults are caught up in the wishes of parents or other older adults without having a real desire to teach. This lack of opportunity to examine options is compounded by the rush to select a major in college. Teachers who are most satisfied in their careers tend to be those who have found a fit between their personalities and teaching.

Educate for Perceptual Clarity. Donald Meichenbaum (1977) and Aaron Beck (1976) have noted the connection between thoughts and feelings. Studies of human behavior suggest that thoughts often determine feelings. Beck has identified several significant ways that people distort their thinking through internal dialogue, often called self-talk (what we say to ourselves and what we hear when we talk to ourselves). There is growing evidence that learning to monitor self-talk and practicing perceptual clarity can be valuable processes for the education of teachers.

Cognitive distortions in self-talk block new learning by reducing the amount of information teachers have to make reasoned decisions. Distorted perceptions result in blocking information that contradicts what we believe to be true about ourselves, others, and the world (Beck & Weishaar, 1989). Teachers are more likely to take risks, recognize achievements, set realistic expectations for themselves and others, and maintain good discipline in classrooms when their perceptual processes are free from distortion.

Conclusion

This chapter has offered several suggestions for the preparation of invitational teachers for next-century schools. Current proposals for reform in education that are limited to academic content or instructional skills do not adequately recognize the necessity for expanding the educative process from cognitive development to affective development, and preparing teachers to recognize and respond to the affective needs of students.

The six specific suggestions for the preparation of teachers of the 21st century are as follows: (a) focus on the teacher of teachers, (b) take an internal frame of reference, (c) select supervising teachers carefully, (d) use group processes frequently, (e) conduct integrative seminars, and (f) provide training for perceptual clarity. Although the six suggestions are not inclusive of all the experiences tomorrow's teachers need, they do focus on the heart of teaching—and that is teaching with the heart. Attempting to improve education without preparing teachers in human relationships is surely a lost cause.

References

Aspy, D., Roebuck, F. N., & Benoit, D. (1987). Person-centered education in the information age. *Person Centered Review, 2*, 87-98.

Beck, A. (1976). *Cognitive therapy and the emotional disorders*. New York: New American Library.

Beck, A., & Weishaar, M. (1989). Cognitive therapy. In A. Freeman, K. Simon, L. Beutler, & H. Arkowitz (Eds.), *Comprehensive handbook of cognitive therapy* (pp. 21-36). New York: Plenum.

Carkhuff, R. P. (1987). *The productive teacher* (Vols. 1 & 2). Amherst, MA: Human Resources Press.

Cazden, C., & Mehan, H. (1989). Principles from sociology and anthropology: Context, code, classroom and culture. In M. Reynolds (Ed.), *Knowledge base for the beginning teacher* (pp. 47-57). Oxford, UK: Pergamon.

Cohen, R. M. (1991). *A lifetime of teaching: Portraits of five veteran high school teachers*. New York: Teachers College Press.

Combs, A. W., Soper, D. W., Gooding, C. T., Benton, J. A., Dickman, J. F., & Usher, R. H. (1969). *Florida studies in the helping professions* (Social Science Monograph No. 37). Gainesville: University of Florida Press.

Kagan, D. M. (1992). Professional growth among preservice and beginning teachers. *Review of Educational Research, 62,* 129-169.

Louden, W. (1991). *Understanding teaching: Continuity and change in teachers' knowledge*. New York: Teachers College Press.

Meichenbaum, D. (1977). *Cognitive behavior modification: An integrative approach*. New York: Plenum.

Mizer, J. E. (1964). Cipher in the snow. *NEA Journal, 53,* 8-10.

Patterson, C. H. (1985). *The therapeutic relationship*. New York: Brooks/Cole.

Purkey, W. W., & Novak, J. (1984). *Inviting school success: A self-concept approach to teaching* (2nd ed.). Belmont, CA: Wadsworth.

Purkey, W. W., & Novak, J. (1995). *Inviting school success: A self-concept approach to teaching* (3rd ed.). Belmont, CA: Wadsworth.

Purkey, W. W., & Stanley, P. H. (1991). *Invitational teaching, learning and living*. Washington, DC: National Educational Association.

Rogers, C. R. (1957). The necessary and sufficient conditions of therapeutic personality change. *Journal of Consulting Psychology, 21,* 95-103.

Rogers, C. R. (1961). *On becoming a person*. Boston: Houghton Mifflin.

Whitman, N., Spendlove, D., & Clark, C. (1986). *Increasing students' learning: A faculty guide to reducing stress among students* (ASHE-ERIC Higher Education Report No. 4). Washington, DC: ASHE-ERIC.

❖ 2 ❖

Supervising Student Teachers

A New Paradigm

MARVIN A. HENRY

In most situations requiring supervision in the teaching profession, evaluation is the main objective. The supervisor is probably the building administrator, and the focus is on ensuring quality or securing evidence to make recommendations for continuation as a teacher. During student teaching, however, supervision takes on a different perspective that requires the cooperating teacher to be both supervisor and evaluator. This chapter addresses how a supervising teacher can prepare for this dual role. Effectively evaluating, while simultaneously encouraging a student to move in a few short weeks from a college student to an independent professional, is not easy.

No other professional role duplicates that of the cooperating teacher, because that person must be both supervisor and evaluator. Teaching responsibilities must be relinquished in order to provide a laboratory where a student teacher can develop. Additionally, the cooperating teacher works in virtual isolation from other supervisors. The only contact with other supervisors or professionals will probably be with college or university personnel, who will make an occasional visit or phone call. In many cases there are no specific requirements for being a cooperating teacher, nor is any training either required or available for this critical role.

Student teaching supervision is a unique activity that requires adjustment in thinking so that the traditional nature of supervision is tempered by the need for growth. Supervisors must make judgments about when and whether the student teacher should be supervised or evaluated. More important, the student teacher must understand whether the method is supervision or evaluation. Decisions must be made about the appropriate procedures to use for observation and conferencing. This chapter will outline the fundamentals regarding the above concerns and offer concrete suggestions for being both a supervisor and an evaluator.

Necessary Conditions for Supervision and Evaluation to Exist Simultaneously

A cooperating teacher must balance the roles of supervisor and evaluator. As an evaluator, a cooperating teacher must look for indicators that will support a summary judgment of student teaching performance. This judgment may be the only formal procedure used to determine whether a student teacher has performed successfully.

The role of evaluator implies summative judgment based on identifiable criteria. Although supervision and evaluation are similar in some respects, there are significant differences overall. Supervision is collegial and formative, focusing on such factors as classroom interaction, instruction, and student learning. Evaluation is based on judgment from a superior and is summative in nature. It concentrates on such factors as quality control and effective performance on a predetermined set of criteria. It serves as documentation for administrative decisions, which, in the case of student teachers, are the determination of a grade.

Unfortunately, the role of evaluator presents conditions that can hinder the student teacher's professional growth if the teacher is regarded as a professional superior who has the power to determine the fate of the neophyte teacher. Such a role can create suspicion and apprehension on the part of the student teacher in spite of efforts to downplay the significance of the role.

A cooperating teacher must work around this hindrance to provide a daily program of formative growth for the student teacher. This involves such familiar supervisory procedures as providing objective analysis of a lesson, conferencing, structuring in-class and out-of-class experiences, and constantly urging the student teacher to engage in reflection.

It is little wonder, then, that student teachers cited relationships with their cooperating teachers as a major area of difficulty (Zerr, 1988). Henry (Henry & Beasley, 1989) observed that personal relationships included personal adjustments, adjustment to students, and adjusting to the personality of the cooperating teacher. One can readily see that the supervisory position would be much different from an evaluative stance in dealing with these categories.

Cole (1993) presented a paper regarding problems and paradoxes in beginning teacher support that seem to have implications for student teacher supervision. Issues included balancing the conflicting roles of teacher support and evaluation, and treading the fine line between development and intervention.

It is difficult to accept the challenge of simultaneously being a helper and an evaluator. Although some would argue that a supervisor cannot accomplish this, thousands of experiences have shown that a cooperating teacher can perform both functions. A supervisor can be both a helper and evaluator if three conditions exist:

1. Trust has been established. If a cooperating teacher and student teacher can successfully establish a relationship of mutual trust, a student teacher will be more likely to accept a cooperating teacher as both supervisor and evaluator. Moreover, the cooperating teacher will also likely be more comfortable with both roles.

2. Different criteria are used for supervision and evaluation. Because supervision and evaluation differ, distinct criteria need to be used so that the purpose of the contact will be clear.

3. The student teacher knows which role the supervisor is performing. A procedure is more readily accepted and likely to be successful if the student teacher understands whether the cooperating teacher is supervising or evaluating.

Determining the Best Approaches for Supervision and Evaluation

Carl Glickman (1990) proposes that different supervisory approaches should be taken depending upon the developmental level of the person being supervised. This level is determined by assessing teachers' level of abstraction and commitment. The following represents the author's application of Glickman's ideas specifically to the process of supervising and evaluating student teachers.

The abstraction, or conceptual, level ranges from low conceptual abilities to highly abstract skills. Persons with low levels of abstraction may be characterized by such factors as the inability to see more than one alternative to a problem, or by tending to blame problems on external forces. Student teachers at low levels, for example, might be inclined to stereotype students or say that "everything" has been tried and nothing is working. When queried, they may admit having tried only one or two approaches and may not recognize that there are alternative processes. In other words, student teachers with low abstraction think in concrete and limited terms.

Persons with high abstraction are more able to discriminate, differentiate, and integrate. They are less rigid and see more alternatives to a question or teaching problem. Whereas persons at low levels of abstraction may resort to lecturing and asking low-level questions, persons who are higher in abstract ability will be more likely to take risks, explore ideas, and encourage students to be creative and express themselves. Teachers with high levels of abstraction are more likely both to see that differences exist among pupils and to use a variety of teaching models.

Persons also vary in their levels of commitment. Student teachers at low levels appear to be indifferent and perhaps even lazy. They see teaching as a job rather than as a profession, are inclined to be satisfied with minimum standards only, and have little or no commitment to the profession.

At the other end of the continuum is a high level of commitment. These persons are committed to the students they teach and are eager to make their teaching more effective. They normally are high energy persons who plan to make a career in teaching.

The more effective supervisor will determine the developmental level of the student teacher in order to determine the most effective process for growth. Glickman identifies four quadrants for a frame of reference in making the decision:

1. *Quadrant One—Low Commitment and Low Abstraction.* This person has difficulty defining problems and knows fewer ways of responding to them. A student teacher in this quadrant is the one most likely not to go into teaching, or to remain there for only a short period of time. The Quadrant One student teacher has little concern for students, sees teaching as a job to be performed, and usually thinks in concrete terms, where there is only one solution or an easy answer to a problem. Students are categorized rather than considered to be unique. This person will likely be unimaginative or unconcerned about teaching. There is little variation in teaching technique, and this technique will probably be a conventional or traditional style. He or she is often one of the first persons leaving the school at the end of the day.

2. *Quadrant Two—High Commitment and Low Abstraction.* The Quadrant Two student teacher may be eager but lack a sense of direction. High on commitment, this person will devote an endless amount of energy to the job, but this energy will likely not be coupled with a definable purpose. The problem is not desire; it is a lack of abstraction. This person may have a lot of ideas but lacks the ability to pursue them, to carry them out, or to discriminate between those that work and those that will not.

3. Quadrant Three—High Abstraction and Low Commitment. The student teacher in this category will be highly intelligent but have a lack of concern for teaching. He or she may verbalize what can or should be done but does not follow through. Because of low motivation, progress toward acceptable levels of teacher competency is slow to develop, or virtually nonexistent. This individual is a thinker but not a doer.

4. Quadrant Four—High Abstraction and High Commitment. A student teacher at this level of development will be rare but is the type of student teacher one hopes would be entering the profession. The person will demonstrate high intellectual capacity, will see students as unique individuals, will be aware of alternative teaching strategies, and will be willing to try techniques that involve some risks. Furthermore, this person will be enthusiastic about and dedicated to the teaching profession. He or she will likely have been active in student professional activities and will try to take advantage of every opportunity that student teaching has to offer.

Determining Levels of Development

Student teachers cannot be neatly placed into one of the above quadrants; most will be on a continuum from low to high. It is necessary to make some judgments in order to determine the best supervisory or evaluative approach. In order to categorize the student teacher, a supervisor may want to employ one or more of the following options:

1. Inquire about the student teacher. A good source should be the information form that accompanies the application for assignment. Notice the academic level of the student and study the types of classes taken. Look at the activities that the student has been involved in. Are they numerous? Are they good training materials for becoming a professional? Finally, look at any written statements the student may have made. Are there any indications of commitment or abstraction there?

2. Talk with the student teacher. Initial conferences can often reveal a student's orientation. During the conversation look for the student teacher's ability to make abstract statements. Pose hypothetical questions and see what the responses are. Describe your expectations for the projected workload in order to observe the student teacher's response.

3. Observe the student teacher. Note the pattern of behaviors and actions. How does he or she relate to pupils on an individual level? How is discretionary time spent? What kinds of questions are asked? What nonverbal cues do you get when you see the student teacher interact with pupils and adults?

Patterns should begin to emerge as the supervisor observes and analyzes. From those patterns, a supervisor can identify the predominant level of development and then determine the best approach for supervision and evaluation.

Supervisory Styles for Different Quadrants

Once the developmental level has been determined, a decision must be made about the supervisory or evaluative approach to be taken. The style chosen must match the developmental level of the individual being supervised or evaluated in order to ensure growth.

Supervision and Evaluation
of the Quadrant One Student Teacher

The Quadrant One student teacher may need to be both motivated and informed. In this situation the supervisor can assume that the student teacher needs a structured response. The procedure most likely to succeed would be a directive control model, where the supervisor gives instructions and standardizes expectations. This model is characterized by the supervisor telling the student teacher what should be done and describing the indicators for success. For example, a supervisor might say, "John,

I want you to spend a minimum of 15 minutes in class tomorrow questioning students about their understanding of the assignment and having them draw conclusions about its relationship to the previous unit. You should conclude by listing the major ideas on the board."

If the supervisor decides to take an evaluative stance for a Quadrant One student teacher, he or she might review the lesson and indicate whether it was successful according to specified criteria. This could be followed by a listing of expectations for the next lesson.

Supervising and Evaluating
the Quadrant Two Student Teacher

The Quadrant Two student teacher may need a different type of directive supervision. Whereas the Quadrant One student teacher may benefit from directive control procedures, directive informational procedures may be used for the Quadrant Two student teacher. These differ from directive control in that the supervisor presents choices and allows the student teacher to make the decision from those choices. Control still rests with the supervisor because of the options presented, but the student teacher has some autonomy to make a selection. In a directive informational situation, a supervisor may say, "You can either have students demonstrate their ideas by creating a model on newsprint, work in groups to explore each other's ideas, or present case studies and ask them to analyze them and relate them to their own experience." In this case the supervisor would be filling in the vacuum of low abstraction ability by providing ideas. The highly motivated student teacher would then be willing to expend the energy to see that the more complex activities are accomplished.

Evaluation of the Quadrant Two student teacher could take the form of providing a limited frame of reference for the student teacher and then asking for analysis. A supervisor might say, "I would rate you as needing more volume in your voice, needing better organization at the beginning of class, and needing to spend more time on task. Which are you going to begin with and what improvement will you try to make by tomorrow?"

Supervising and Evaluating
the Quadrant Three Student Teacher

Student teachers at this level can define a problem and think through possible solutions. A supervisor may want to present a collaborative style at this point. Collaborative supervision occurs when both parties present ideas and negotiate possible solutions. The suggestions will be examined in a collegial manner, and the decision will be one that is mutually determined. The student teacher might present a thought or two followed by suggestions from the supervisor. The ideas will be examined and discussed, and both parties will agree on a course of action.

Evaluating the Quadrant Three student teacher would involve both parties offering a critique and then negotiating any differences. The conclusion would be one that is mutually determined.

Supervising and Evaluating
the Quadrant Four Student Teacher

The best style of supervision for this unusual student is an indirect approach. Because the student teacher can think of problems from many perspectives and generate a variety of alternative plans, a supervisor's role is one of support and encouragement. Questions like, "How are you going to introduce the concept?" or "Have you thought about something really different and exciting for this class?" would be appropriate. The supervisor takes on a supportive role and encourages the student teacher to be creative through questions and interest.

By the same token, the supervisor would provide evaluation through thoughtful questions that cause the student teacher to be more thorough in self-analysis. An example might be something like, "Why are you successful in motivation?"

Making It Work

A supervisor who recognizes the difference between supervision and evaluation, diagnoses the developmental level of student teachers, and understands that different types of supervision are needed is well on the way to being successful. The next step is to put it all together into a program that is understandable to all parties concerned and leads to growth of the student teacher. Consider the following guidelines for making effective student teacher supervision work.

1. Provide effective feedback. According to Freiberg et al. (1987), systematic feedback from a classroom analysis system, self-analysis, and collegial feedback and support are effective for improving student teachers' classroom instruction. Feedback provides objective information that can lead to interpretation of a lesson. In a directive mode, the supervisor would provide concrete information from some kind of analysis sheet or evaluation form. A collaborative supervisor may provide the same type of information but would invite the student teacher to join in the interpretation. The ensuing discussion would conclude with a consensus on the nature of the lesson. A nondirective supervisor would encourage the student teacher to reflect and draw his or her own conclusions about the nature of the lesson.

2. Criteria for supervision and evaluation should be known and applied in an understandable manner. A review of studies by Thomson (1992) found that the more familiar student teachers are with competency-based assessment measures and the more exposure they have to self-assessment and assessment by supervising teachers, the more competent they will be in class. Supervisory weaknesses were found to occur when supervisors were unable to connect specific teacher behaviors with student outcomes and to distinguish effective from ineffective instruction. A lack of consistency among appraisers as to what is effective, and the persistence of an adversarial rather than a collaborative relationship between supervisor and supervisee, were also problems (Crisci et al., 1991). If the supervisor is uncertain about using analysis or evaluative procedures and the criteria are unknown to the student teacher, there will likely be resistance and little progress. Criteria should be explained, discussed, and agreed upon before an analysis or evaluation occurs.

3. The supervisor must be skilled in observation techniques and conferencing. Role behaviors are closely related to teaching tasks (Stahlhut et al., 1988). Supervisors and student teachers need time to discuss personal and professional concerns throughout the clinical experience; supervisors must be effective and skillful in management and teaching techniques so that a student teacher can be coached through observation, discussion, and modeling; and supervisors need to critique student teacher behaviors in a positive manner. Communication skills and goal identification are important, but teachers need to be able to observe, collect data, conference with an adult, and ask reflective questions (Cromwell, 1991). Cooperating teachers should be caring, active listeners, sensitive to the views of others, and should offer candid, regular feedback in a supportive manner (Enz & Cook, 1991).

4. Stress good human relationships. Effective personal relationships are critical to all elements in the supervisory process. Zerr (1988) identified six categories of how supervising teachers helped establish good relationships. These included (a) personal influence of supervisors, (b) aid and encouragement, (c) help with initiation into teaching, (d) help in assuming additional responsibility for class, (e) suggestions for improving plans, sources of materials, etc., and (f) guidance with classroom management and professional growth. Conversely, lack of substantive communication was found to provide barriers to improved student teaching supervision (Kauffman, 1992).

The above conditions are not natural gifts nor are they developed through casual experience. If student teachers are to significantly improve during their practicum experience, it is essential to adequately train the cooperating teacher (Melnick, 1989). Training in all aspects of supervision is necessary. Some institutions offer courses in the supervision of student teaching; others offer workshops or in-service sessions. A course in the supervision of instruction or the supervision of student teachers or a good book in the area should be minimum requirements for a cooperating teacher.

Conclusion

The new paradigm for supervision suggested in this chapter may simply be a review of the obvious. Supervision and evaluation are two different processes, but they can be exercised by one person if certain conditions exist. The success of any student teacher depends on accurate diagnosis of the developmental level of the student and the application of the appropriate supervisory behaviors. In order to be effective in supervision, a cooperating teacher must display effective human relations skills, be competent in human relationships, and know various methods for providing meaningful feedback.

References

Cole, A. (1993, April). *Problems and paradoxes in beginning teacher support: Issues concerning school administrators.* Paper presented at the annual meeting of the American Educational Research Association, Atlanta.

Crisci, P. E., et al. (1991, April). *Using the current paradigms in teacher training to prepare principals and mentor teachers to appraise classroom instruction.* Paper presented at the annual meeting of the American Association of Colleges of Teacher Education, Atlanta. (ERIC No. ED 333 544)

Cromwell, R. R. (1991). *Key supervision skills that will touch the future of school reform.* (ERIC No. ED 352 355)

Enz, B. J., & Cook, S. J. (1991, April). *Student teachers' and cooperating teachers' perspectives of mentoring functions: Harmony or dissonance?* Paper presented at the annual meeting of the American Educational Research Association, San Francisco.

Freiberg, H. J., et al. (1987, February). *Improving the quality of student teaching.* Paper presented at the national meeting of the Association of Teacher Educators, Houston.

Glickman, C. (1990). *Supervision of instruction: A developmental approach* (2nd ed.). Needham Heights, MA: Allyn & Bacon.

Henry, M. A., & Beasley, W. W. (1989). *Supervising student teachers the professional way* (4th ed.). Terre Haute, IN: Sycamore Press.

Kauffman, D. (1992, February). *Supervision of student teachers* (ERIC Clearinghouse on Teacher Education No. SP 033773).

Melnick, S. A. (1989, March). *Cooperating teachers: What do they see in the classroom?* Paper presented at the annual meeting of the American Education Research Association, San Francisco.

Stahlhut, R., et al. (1988, February). *Coaching student teachers to elicit mentor role behaviors from their cooperating teachers.* Paper presented at the annual meeting of the American Association of Colleges for Teacher Education, New Orleans.

Thomson, W. S. (1992). *Using videotape as a supplement to traditional student teacher supervision.* (ERIC No. ED 357 014)

Zerr, R. G. (1988, February). *What supervisors of student teaching and student teachers tell us about student teaching.* Paper presented at the American Association of Colleges for Teacher Education, New Orleans.

Assimilating
the Culture of Teaching

The Student Teaching Experience

PATRICIA T. WHITFIELD

Student teaching has historically been the capstone experience of teacher preparation programs (Guyton & McIntire, 1990; Johnson & Yates, 1982). The opportunity to work in "real" schools with and as "real" teachers eclipses all other program components (Bolin, 1990). Generally, teacher educators expect candidates to integrate theory with practice and begin to become professionals dedicated to lifelong learning. School people expect candidates to learn the culture of schools and life as teachers. These differing perspectives coexist, leading to several questions related to the process of assimilating the culture of teaching. How is that culture defined, to what extent and in what ways do candidates assimilate the culture of teaching, and how does the assimilation process impact the candidate?

Feiman-Nemser and Floden (1986) advocated considering the *cultures*, rather than the *culture*, of teaching. Teachers need to make sense of their work. This chapter will emphasize the particular culture of teaching that relates to learning the tasks, roles, relationships, and responsibilities associated with assuming greater accountability in the education of children.

My experience as a teacher educator indicates that the most effective student teachers are those who have been most successful at "sense making." Skill in deciphering school cultures must be carefully nurtured through program design. Early field experiences augmented by focused observations, journal writing, and frequent conversations with peers and faculty develop in candidates a keener orientation toward schools and their internal workings.

Candidates' perceptions of teaching change over time, with the preservice component a "fantasy stage" (Ryan, 1986) in which they espouse illusory ideals about what it means to be a teacher, and "individual careers are socially constructed and individually experienced over time" (Ball & Goodson, 1985). Feiman-Nemser, McDiarmid, Melnick, and Parker (1989) determined that "students' conceptions of teaching as an activity grew richer and more complex as a result of [a beginning] education course." A variety of personal, professional, societal, and contextual factors which should be addressed in preparation programs impacts the socialization of candidates.

Occupational socialization must view beginners as active agents in their own professional development, rather than passive recipients of institutional values (Zeichner, 1980). Numerous researchers (Lortie, 1975; Ross, 1987; Zeichner, Tabachnik, & Densmore, 1987) maintain that beginning teachers have years of experience in observing teaching behaviors in their own education, mitigated by their professional preparation, which combine to create "cognitively mapped prior experiences" (Gearing, 1976).

One program with which I was associated effectively implemented a socializing strategy to transform novices into active agents. Each semester students met with their advisers to assess their progress in program outcomes and identified "what I need to know now that will make me a better teacher." Afterward, faculty related students' perceived professional development needs to the program model and designed appropriate learning modules. Students actively involved in their own curriculum design were socialized to a collaborative, empowering model, intended to foster a greater sense of autonomy.

By the end of the preparation program candidates should move from a perception of self as "student" to that of "teacher," a paradigm shift essential for the novice to assimilate the culture of teaching and begin a career-long process of professional growth. The candidate moves from passive to active, from a lesser to a greater sense of efficacy. One student teacher (Whitfield, 1990) described this evolution in her journal as "a continual growing experience. Working right in the classroom, dealing with everyday problems, evaluating student performance, and working with the curriculum has been the most worthwhile part of my education."

Candidates enter the preprofessional passage of student teaching with sets of feelings, perceptions, and motivations—or lack thereof—identified first by Fuller (1969) as concerns that evolve across the span of the teacher preparation curriculum. These concerns evolve from those *unrelated to teaching* through those about *self as teacher* to those about the *teaching act itself*, culminating in those related to the *impact on students*.

Negotiating a new culture requires the ability to read it, a skill developed by diverse classroom experiences provided to candidates and leading to developing rich pedagogical repertoires to apply in student teaching. I was associated with a program that required of candidates numerous field experiences prior to student teaching—inner-city, self-contained, upper socioeconomic, and open classrooms, across grade levels. Students participated in weekly seminars that began at entry to the professional program and continued until program completion. In seminar they discussed observations and concerns, and they engaged in healthy dialogue about the cultures of schools. The cross-fertilization of early methods, and student teachers gave candidates the opportunity to perceive themselves as part of a developmental continuum of professional growth.

Teacher educators must help novices forge a professional identity that spans the teacher preparation program and culminates with student teaching. To facilitate the transition from novice to professional, teacher educators must help candidates understand school contextual realities and teach them how to implement appropriate and diverse teaching strategies that consider those realities (Etheridge, 1988). Norton (1976) emphasized that the identification of one's "personal truth" was crucial. Early in preservice education, candidates must learn to recognize what is right for them personally and to eschew the "attractiveness of foreign truths that belong to others" (Dewey, 1904).

High-achieving preservice teachers prefer active involvement in course work, eagerly presenting and defending their ideas to their peers and believing that their participation in intellectual dialogue is the most important goal of a college class (Skipper, 1984). Schön's (1983) ideas on the nature of professional knowledge have emphasized the importance of reflective practice and the possibilities for teacher educators to coach teachers toward reflective teaching.

I've kept a record of the comments of 389 student teachers' perceptions of four areas of concern related to teaching: stress, relationship with cooperating teachers, management/discipline, and sense of competence. These candidates reported stress manifesting as family problems, crying almost every night, poor health, exhaustion, panic, sleep difficulty, and doubt about choosing the right profession.

Confronted with classroom management problems, they struggled with students off task, a loss of control, frustration with cooperating teachers' management systems viewed as negative, a perceived lack of student respect, and unaccustomed moments of personal "temper." In working out less than positive relationships with cooperating teachers, some reported experiencing a lack of support, interference with their own teaching or management, or early abandonment. With regard to competence, students almost universally focused on their emerging sense of efficacy.

Efficacy growth was revealed in their strategies for dealing with the previously mentioned areas of concern. Feedback from seminars and cooperating teachers was identified as helpful in dealing with stress, as were getting more sleep, exercise, and personal time. One individual declared, "I decided I would survive, no matter what. That I might at some point meet up with these in the classroom, that I might need to have had these experiences." Strategies for dealing with management ranged from "trying different methods until something started to change" through being "firm, positive, consistent, and fair" to "taking more time to organize my work area, spending time with the students clarifying my objectives and expected behaviors for the class." Approaches for working with cooperating teachers required "adaptation and flexibility" and "trying to keep a strong sense of my own center and not get shook [sic]," to a very realistic "never did—some communication just never came."

Self-knowledge is essential in bridging cultures and moving from novice to professional. McWhirter and Jeffries (1984) suggested that the following themes be introduced into preservice education to foster introspection and reflectivity in candidates: self-disclosure, trust, competition/cooperation, anxiety and stress, perceptions, feelings, wants and needs, self-fulfilling prophecy, self-esteem, verbal and nonverbal communication, small-group behavior, and personality type. Journals and personal narrative (Borko, Livingston, McCaleb, & Mauro, 1988; Klug, 1983; Pultarek, 1993), structured interviews (Trumbull & Slack, 1991), and seminars (Koskela, 1985) can be especially helpful. Research on self-assessment suggests that people can accurately observe their own behavior and that self-appraisals are at least as effective as other assessment procedures (Graham, 1984).

My own experience with student interactive journals, in which the candidate writes and the faculty member or supervisor comments, has been fruitful in tracking professional growth in novices. Although some candidates resist at first and others may never reach deep levels of reflectivity, journals have been both helpful in chronicling their emerging professional personae and an asset in forestalling impending problems. Designated readers can communicate concerns with significant others in the supervisory and mentoring relationships on the basis of journal entries that become a fail-safe mechanism.

A key factor in assimilating the culture of teaching pertains to candidates' abilities to use student cues in determining appropriate teaching strategies (Kagan & Tippins, 1991). Within student teaching, candidates should be helped to develop observational skills for identifying exemplary practice of cooperating teachers and self-assessment strategies for evaluating their own successes and failures in monitoring student feedback. Borko, Lalik, and Tomchin (1987) found through examining their journals that student teachers characterized a successful learning environment as one that engaged learners actively.

Much research emphasizes the influence of the cooperating teacher in the shaping of the novice (Funk & Long, 1982; Olsen & Carter, 1989; Scholl, 1990). Thus, the careful selection and preparation of cooperating teachers should be paramount.

The literature on collaboration in education (Ham, 1987; Oja, 1988; Sikula, 1990; Sirotnik & Goodlad, 1990; Theis-Sprinthall & Sprinthall, 1987) addresses the reconceptualization of the role of school-based professionals in teacher education. With the restructuring of both K-12 schools and teacher education, teacher educators enjoy redefined relationships with school-based colleagues, operating in mutual trust and respect, now sharing expertise and responsibility. Exemplary models assign increasing autonomy to teacher mentors specially trained in the supervision of student teachers while teacher educators are spending more "real time" in schools, a situation contributing not only to their professional growth but also to their credibility with candidates.

Student teaching, then, is the structured and supported process of assimilating the culture of teaching related to acquiring a teaching repertoire, developing pedagogical knowledge, and learning roles and responsibilities. Teacher educators can facilitate the process by providing curriculum and experiences rich in knowledge about and actual experiences with schools, augmented by frequent opportunities for students to reflect and develop a sense of efficacy. Redefined roles for teacher educators and school-based colleagues enable candidates to experience an aspect of school culture more appropriate for the 21st century—a collegial model of continuing professional growth for all parties.

Ultimately, student teaching is a pivotal point between the individual as student and the individual as teacher (Progoff, 1975). The student teacher who is taught to reflect on teaching will be the one who carries a legacy of excellence to the future of our profession (Dewey, 1904).

References

Ball, S., & Goodson, I. (1985). Understanding teachers: Concepts and contexts. In S. J. Ball & I. F. Goodson (Eds.), *Teachers' lives and careers* (pp. 1-26). Philadelphia: Falmer.

Bolin, F. (1990). Helping student teachers think about teaching: Another look at Lou. *Journal of Teacher Education, 41*(1), 10-19.

Borko, H., Lalik, E., & Tomchin, E. (1987). Student teachers' understandings of successful and unsuccessful student teaching. *Teaching and Teacher Education, 3*(2), 77-90.

Borko, H., Livingston, C., McCaleb, J., & Mauro, L. (1988). *Student teachers' planning and post-lesson reflections: Patterns and implications for teacher preparation.* Paper presented at the annual meeting of the American Educational Research Association.

Dewey, J. (1904). The relation of theory to practice in education. In C. A. McMurry (Ed.), *The relation of theory to practice in the education of teachers* (Third yearbook of the national society for the scientific study of education: Part I) (pp. 9-30). Chicago: University of Chicago Press.

Etheridge, C. P. (1988, November). *Socialization on the job: How beginning teachers move from university learnings to school-based practices.* Paper presented at the meeting of the Mid-South Educational Research Association, Louisville, KY.

Feiman-Nemser, S., & Floden, R. (1986). The cultures of teaching. In M. Wittrock (Ed.), *Handbook of research on teaching* (pp. 505-525). New York: Macmillan.

Feiman-Nemser, S., McDiarmid, G., Melnick, S., & Parker, M. (1989). *Changing beginning teachers' conceptions: A description of an introductory teacher education course* (Research Report No. 89-1). East Lansing, MI: The National Center for Research on Teacher Education.

Fuller, F. (1969). Concerns of teachers: A developmental conceptualization. *American Educational Research Journal, 6*(2), 207-226.

Funk, F., & Long, B. (1982). The cooperating teacher as most significant other: A competent humanist. *Action in Teacher Education, 4*(2), 57-64.

Gearing, F. O. (1976). Steps toward a general theory of cultural transmission. In J. I. Roberts & S. Akinsaya (Eds.), *Educational patterns and cultural configurations*. New York: David McKay.

Graham, S. (1984, Fall). Teachers' self-assessment of their instructional competence: An evaluation of special education preservice programs. *College Student Journal, 18*, 236-245.

Guyton, E., & McIntire, J. (1990). Student teaching and school experiences. In W. R. Houston (Ed.), *Handbook of research on teacher education* (pp. 514-534). New York: Macmillan.

Ham, M. C. (1987). Enhancing supervisory effectiveness through collaborative action research. *Peabody Journal of Education, 64*(2), 44-56.

Johnson, J., & Yates, J. (1982). *A national survey of student teaching programs* (ERIC Document Reproduction Service No. ED 232 963). DeKalb: Northern Illinois University.

Kagan, D., & Tippins, D. (1991). Helping student teachers attend to student cues. *The Elementary School Journal, 91*(4), 343-356.

Klug, B. (1983). *Promises to keep: An ethnographic study of supervision of preservice teachers*. Doctoral dissertation, University of Cincinnati.

Koskela, R. (1985). *A search for reflective thought in the student teaching seminar. A case study*. Doctoral dissertation, University of Wisconsin, Madison.

Lortie, D. (1975). *School teacher: A sociological study*. Chicago: University of Chicago Press.

McWhirter, J., & Jeffries, J. (1984). Career awareness and self-exploration (CASE) groups: A self-assessment model for career decision-making. *The Personnel and Guidance Journal, 62*, 580-582.

Norton, D. L. (1976). *Personal destinies: A philosophy of ethical individualism*. Princeton, NJ: Princeton University Press.

Oja, S. N. (1988). *Some promising endeavors in school-university collaboration: Collaborative research and collaborative supervision in a five-year teacher education program* (ERIC Document Reproduction Service No. SP 029867). Paper presented at a National Holmes Group meeting.

Olsen, P., & Carter, K. (1989). The capabilities of cooperating teachers in USA schools for communicating knowledge about teaching. *Journal of Education for Teaching, 15*(2), 113-131.

Progoff, I. (1975). *At a journal workshop: The basic text and guide for using the intensive journal process.* New York: Dialogue House Library.

Pultarek, E. (1993). Facilitating reflective thought in novice teachers. *Journal of Teacher Education, 44*(4), 288-295.

Ross, E. W. (1987). Teacher perspective development: A study of preservice social studies teachers. *Theory and Research in Social Education, 15*(4), 225-243.

Ryan, K. (1986). *The induction of new teachers.* Bloomington, IN: Phi Delta Kappa Educational Foundation.

Scholl, R. (1990). *University supervisor: Circuit rider or teacher educator.* Paper presented at the meeting of the Association of Teacher Educators, Las Vegas, NV.

Schön, D. (1983). *The reflective practitioner.* New York: Basic Books.

Sikula, J. (1990). National commission reports of the 1980's. In W. Houston (Ed.), *Handbook of research on teacher education.* New York: Macmillan.

Sirotnik, K., & Goodlad, J. (Eds.). (1990). *School-university partnerships in action.* New York: Teachers College Press.

Skipper, C. E. (1984, Winter). Preferred instructional modes and course goals of high-achieving preservice teachers. *College Student Journal*, 397-400.

Theis-Sprinthall, L., & Sprinthall, N. (1987). Experienced teachers: Agents for revitalization and renewal mentors and teacher educators. *Journal of Teacher Education, 169*(1), 65-75.

Trumbull, D., & Slack, M. (1991). Learning to ask, listen, and analyze: Using structured interviewing assignments to develop reflection in preservice science teachers. *International Journal of Science Education, 13*(2), 129-142.

Whitfield, P. (1990). *Redesigning the student teaching seminar as a vehicle for forging professional identity in the novice.* Paper presented at the meeting of the Association of Teacher Educators, Las Vegas, NV.

Zeichner, K. (1980). Myths and realities: Field-based experiences in preservice teacher education. *Journal of Teacher Education, 31*(6), 45-54.

Zeichner, K., Tabachnik, B., & Densmore, K. (1987). Individual, institutional, and cultural influences on the development of teachers' craft knowledge. In J. Calderhead (Ed.), *Exploring teachers' thinking* (pp. 21-59). London: Cassell.

Communication

The Key to Successful Field Experiences

MARGARET H. SHAW-BAKER

All communication requires two basic things: a speaking voice and a listening ear. Communication does not occur otherwise. Herein lies the key to successful field experiences. Without communication, there is no supervision in field experiences, for supervision is a process of communicating. Effective communication results in the best of field experiences; a breakdown in communication can result in the worst of field experiences.

Responsibilities of the
Field Experience Triad in Communicating

Generally there are three persons involved in any field experience situation: the cooperating classroom teacher, the student teacher, and the university supervisor. Each has a responsibility to be an effective communicator.

The responsibilities of cooperating teachers include communicating to the children that the student teacher is to be viewed and respected as a second teacher in the classroom, rather than a student or helper. They must aid the student teacher in quickly becoming familiar with the class curriculum by communicating immediate goals and long-range objectives at an orientation conference. Throughout the student teaching semester, cooperating teachers discuss curricular issues before and after a lesson is taught, allow the student teacher to experiment with various teaching methods and techniques, and provide the student teacher with both verbal and written feedback, sharing basic strengths as well as areas that need improvement. Cooperating teachers complete all formal evaluations required by the university and share their formative and summative assessments with the student teacher and the university supervisor. They must communicate with the university supervisor if the student teacher is unable to do the required work.

The responsibilities of student teachers include communicating with the classroom cooperating teacher, the building principal, and the university supervisor regarding roles and expectations during the experience. They share with both the cooperating teacher and the university supervisor their insights into the fundamental processes of learning, teaching, and assessing their pupils, as well as reflections on their own learnings and problem-solving strategies.

The university supervisor is a member of the university faculty and serves as the liaison between the university and the schools that cooperate with the student teaching program. University supervisors work directly with both the student teacher and the cooperating teacher. Their responsibilities include communicating the university expectations and formulating the general plan for the student teaching experience. They observe the student teachers in a teaching environment and are prepared to offer constructive suggestions for continued growth and improvement. They confer with both student teachers and the cooperating teachers regarding the student teacher's progress and provide assistance as concerns arise during student teaching. University supervisors have the responsibility of assigning a final grade after consultation with the cooperating teacher and the student teacher.

Because we all enter into field experience relationships as persons with different histories, resources, and knowledge, we bring varied perceptions, possibilities, strengths, and weaknesses to these relationships. Our differences have the potential to unite, though too often they do just the opposite. Learning interpersonal communication skills must accompany learning acceptance of human differences. Many of our differences are personality differences.

Personality Differences in Communicating

Psychologists have long recognized that there are basic personality differences among human beings. Our personality differences affect the way we communicate, in both transmitting and receiving verbal and nonverbal meanings. In some cases, we have personality and communication matches; in other cases, our personality differences can become resources for allowing us to see things from another perspective. Myers and Myers (1980) provide a psychological type framework for us to examine some of these similarities and differences. This framework is useful in helping us maximize our communicative competence, allowing more productive communication among all parties involved in field experiences.

Extroversion and Introversion. Student teachers come to us as extroverts and introverts, just as supervisors are also extroverted and introverted. Extroverts are energized by all the stimulating events bombarding them throughout the day. They need relationships and get their best ideas by bouncing them off their peers, their cooperating teacher, and the children. Those who are learning by bouncing their ideas off the children as they teach may be doing more talking than the children. Their explanations may be too wordy, lacking the focus of key points through their myriad of details. They may not be listening to the children. They act, then maybe reflect upon their actions. In conflict situations, their preference is to talk it out; the more they talk, the louder and more excited they get. They have difficulty listening; they are just waiting to get their next words out.

Introverts, on the other hand, are stimulated by their inner thoughts and reflections. They need periods of privacy to reflect upon their inner resources, and internal experiences to convey their best ideas. Because they are rehearsing inside their heads, they may not be telling the children enough to make them comfortable with the lesson content. They may be too precise. They reflect and then maybe act upon their thoughts. They are often reserved, quiet, and hard to get to know. They may resent the constant interruptions of the extroverts. In conflict situations, their preference is to privately internalize the situation so they can reflect on what took place. They will rework the dialogue inside their heads, finally deciding what they should have said.

Cooperating teachers also have personality preferences. Where there is a match of preference type, extroverted cooperating teachers and student teachers will thrive on the closeness of the relationship and the tendency of the student teacher to constantly shadow the cooperating teacher. Introverted cooperating teachers and student teachers will recognize the need for each other's privacy and are comfortable with shared quiet work time or working apart from each other. On the other hand, where there is a mixing of preference types, an extroverted student teacher can drive introverted cooperating teachers crazy by constantly being underfoot. Introverted student teachers can cause extroverted cooperating teachers great anxiety by reflecting inside their heads before analyzing a lesson, rather than thinking on their feet. One personality preference is neither better nor worse than the other, merely different. Children in our classrooms need both types for their maximum growth.

Information Gathering. Another difference in the way student teachers, cooperating teachers, and university supervisors communicate is in preference for the way they gather information to inform decision making. Some are very literal in their process of receiving or describing incoming information. They are more inclined to look at specific parts and pieces of information as they build the whole picture one step at a time. They read instructions carefully, noticing details. They are not as concerned about the theory behind an idea, but want the facts to support the practical matters in which they engage. They are our realists who learn from firsthand experiences. These student teachers may tend to see lessons in isolation, with little relationship to others before or after. During lessons, they may focus on factual details to the exclusion of key concepts or generalizations. In conflict situations, they hear literally what is said, rather than any implied meanings. They tend to focus on the immediate symptom, rather than what it may take to cure the whole problem. Once a solution is determined, they will know how to carry it out, step-by-step.

Other student teachers, cooperating teachers, and university supervisors globally gather information to inform their decision making before communicating. These individuals prefer the big picture, seeing patterns and relationships and imagining possibilities. They tend to skip directions, following their intuition. Because they are seeing the big picture, they tend to see the relationships among the curricula. Because they are always seeing new possibilities, they may jump into a lesson anywhere, leaping over steps some children may need to scaffold their concept attainment. Important facts and details of a lesson may be missing. In conflict situations, they hear figuratively what the other person's words mean (or what they think was meant). These individuals can easily see links between cause and effect and can put the symptoms of a problem into the bigger picture, even though they may have difficulty implementing the solution.

Making Decisions. A third difference in the way human beings communicate is through our preference for making decisions about the information we gather to solve our problems. Some university supervisors, cooperating teachers, and student teachers weigh the information and decide upon a plan of action based upon logical, objective consideration. Their spontaneous analysis will find the flaws in a plan in advance, yet they are perceived as being highly critical of others. They are concerned for truth and justice but tend to ignore the feelings of their students. There may be a noticeable lack of warmth in the teaching style of these student teachers. In conflict situations, these communicators become uncomfortable when the conflict is interpersonal. If they see feelings are hurt, they may be intimidated by the emotions shown.

Other student teachers, cooperating teachers, and university supervisors make decisions about the information they gather to solve problems by analyzing the situation, considering cause and effect of various actions, yet decide their plan of action based upon their personal, subjective values. These communicators strive to maintain harmonious relationships and spontaneously appreciate those about them. They are the mediators and conciliators in our schools who can usually express the right feeling. Theirs is a personal, sympathetic orientation to understanding people; yet, in their need to maintain harmony, they may be perceived as holding inconsistent, wishy-washy standards for all students. In conflict situations, these individuals personalize everything. Any harsh words translate personally. They assume the blame for the conflict or for the events that lead to the conflict. Their preference is to resolve conflicts by ignoring them and hoping they will go away.

Lifestyle. A fourth difference in the way university supervisors, cooperating teachers, and student teachers communicate is their preference for establishing their lifestyle. Some prefer to organize their lives in a planned and orderly manner. These individuals are most comfortable with preplanned schedules and routines. They like having things decided and settled and they need closure. However, these novice student teachers may not always have considered all or the most important information before reaching a decision. They may not understand the need for flexibility in teaching in the busy school community when an unplanned event occurs. They may have difficulty understanding why their 9:30 a.m. lesson was bumped or moved to a later time in the day. They find too much unstructured time frustrating. In conflict situations, these university supervisors, cooperating teachers, and student teachers strive for control. They may look for someone to blame, sounding tougher than they really are. They are sure they are right; therefore, others must be wrong.

teacher candidates' own solutions for improving their instructional performance in *nondirective supervision*. The supervisory role is to serve as a sounding board. University supervisors or cooperating teachers withhold their own input, verify accuracy of the solutions, elicit information without value judgment, and encourage student teachers' explanations of their position. They do this by listening actively for the purpose of understanding not only what is said but also the perceptions of the student teachers. Active listening includes making eye contact; nodding the head; summarizing the message and the feelings that have been heard, as in, "I understand that you are saying . . . "; and encouraging and acknowledging responses such as, "Yes, I'm following. Tell me more." It also includes matching physical posture and gesture, as well as matching voice tone and rate to build rapport and trust.

The nondirective supervisory approach is best used when the student teacher has many experiences and resources to draw upon. The university supervisor or cooperating teacher must be confident in those abilities. A large block of time is required in this approach, because its success lies in the ability of the student teachers to generate several possible causes of the instructional need, as well as several possible solutions. Finally, student teachers must be trusted to follow through on the plan of action generated for improvement of their instructional behaviors.

The communication behaviors of problem solving, sharing, brainstorming, compromising, consensus, negotiating, teamwork, and mutual goal setting are characteristic of *collaborative supervision*. The university supervisor's and cooperating teacher's role in guiding the conference is to first actively listen to the teacher candidates' reflections by asking how they felt about the lesson, what went well, what they did to bring that about, and what was disappointing. Next, university supervisors and/or cooperating teachers present their own position, describing it in terms of its impact on themselves. "In my own experience . . . " and "It is my belief . . . " are examples of "I" messages. This communication behavior is less likely to be perceived as a complaint or a criticism of the teacher candidate. Once both positions have been clarified, a list of possible solutions is generated by both parties involved. The discussion is then moved to an examination of each other's

ideas, looking for commonalities as well as differences. Consequences of each proposed action are discussed, narrowing the
choices and negotiating a compromise for a mutually acceptable
plan.

The collaborative supervisory approach is best used when
there really are mutually acceptable multiple alternatives to instructional needs. The cooperating teacher must be able to accept
the student teacher as an equal in making instructional decisions.
The student teacher may have many ideas about curriculum,
discipline, and evaluation issues, but may have difficulty formal-
izing a plan of action in the classroom setting. This is an ideal
opportunity for a collaborative supervisory approach.

The communication behaviors of presenting, clarifying, con-
trolling, directing, standardizing, and reinforcing are characteristic of *directive supervision*. The supervisory role in guiding the
conference is to inform, direct, and assess the student teacher's
performance. This direct approach may include reinforcement or
direct instruction in skills or concepts. The university supervisors
or cooperating teachers are responsible for providing the direction
and choices for the teacher candidate. They begin by reviewing
the data collected during the observation, analyzing the results for
the student teacher, and concluding with a plan of action. They
ask for input into the plan, listening to see if the student teacher
understands. If alternatives are necessary or possible, they provide directives for the student teacher to consider before the plan
of action is finalized. Finally, they clarify the details of the plan
along with the rationale, setting up the expected criteria and the
time frame for the plan to be implemented. Possible consequences,
either positive or negative, may need to be discussed, depending
upon the acceptance of the plan by the student teacher. If resistance is met, the broken record method of communication can be
used to repeat the plan: "I understand that you do not agree, but
I want you to. . . ." Expectations are clearly conveyed to student
teachers in the directive approach to supervision.

The directive supervisory approach is best used when time is
short, as in an emergency or crisis situation, or when the student
teacher really has no choice in the matter. These situations would
involve legal issues or school-mandated classroom rules. The

directive approach is best used when student teachers are unable or unwilling to generate alternatives in a more collaborative problem-solving arena. They may be unaware of the need for improvement to be made in the classroom, or they may not have the expertise to identify or solve the instructional problem. These student teachers may have repeatedly failed to follow through on previously formulated courses of action or designated responsibilities.

Summary

The key to successful field experiences is clearly one of communication. Communicative competence in each role in field experience situations—the cooperating classroom teacher, the student teacher, and the university supervisor—requires understanding of the behaviors that enhance or inhibit effective communication. Our perceptions of verbal and nonverbal behaviors may or may not be the intended message of any member of the field experience triad because of our personality differences. We are generally confined in our understanding of others by what we know about ourselves. It follows, then, that a better understanding of ourselves will bring us closer to an understanding of others, allowing more productive communication. We then have at our disposal a choice among varying styles of supervision that is more responsive to the concerns among all parties involved in field experiences.

References

Acheson, K. A., & Gall, M. D. (1992). *Techniques in the clinical supervision of teachers: Preservice and inservice applications.* White Plains, NY: Longman.

Glickman, C. D. (1990). *Supervision of instruction: A developmental approach.* Needham Heights, MA: Allyn & Bacon.

Myers, I. B., & Myers, P. B. (1980). *Gifts differing.* Palo Alto, CA: Consulting Psychologists Press.

❖ 5 ❖

Student Teaching

A Student Teacher's View

LESLEY PEEBLES FAIRLEY

Although the study of pedagogy is often viewed as having a limited importance for teachers, classroom experience has been seen as an essential part of the heart of preparation (Lanier & Little, 1993). This essential part of a student's academic pilgrimage to professionalism is the period of careful thought and reflection on scholarship. Throughout the program, plans for a student's academic course work, ideas, methods, techniques, and approaches to best teach children are introduced, modeled, and experienced, with fellow colleagues as the audience. With this abundance of information gathered from the university classroom, field experience becomes a course for practicing the acquired collection of mental information. The philosophy that "practice makes perfect" holds steadfast as the purpose for teacher education. Whatever the values of the teacher education program, it is held to be through actual practice that one really learns to teach (Bowyer & Van Dyke, 1986). One of the most vital elements of my student teaching experiences was the requirement to participate in both upper-grade-level and lower-grade-level teaching placements. By experiencing two grade levels, my fellow student teachers and I were not locked into a particular level or subject area, and therefore we received a variety of models with a medley of different classroom environments. The more elaborate the experiences were, the more valuable the practice.

One of the most effective means of understanding the feelings of a student teacher's view of this clinical, preservice experience is through the collection of qualitative data. In order to more fully examine the path to professionalism, three teachers' personal accounts of our student teaching experience are discussed, in addition to my own account. The first account is that of the novice student. This is the student waiting in the wings to begin the student teaching field experience, the highlight of his or her academic career. Next, the practitioner student teacher, the student presently active in the field experience program, provides an on-sight account. Then, the mature student teacher, who has just recently completed the field experience portion of the teacher education program, recalls and connects all the academic course work and practicum experience to prepare for needed employment. Finally, the practicing professional implements the experience and knowledge in the honored profession of education.

The novice student, Jeff Nobles, is a current student at The University of Southern Mississippi. As he waits to student teach the fall semester, he claims he is looking forward to getting into the classroom. "I have been gathering materials for my prospective classroom and trying to think of unique ways to present old information," Jeff states as he prepares for his field experience. There are many emotions and thoughts that fill a prospective student teacher's mind. Jeff explains, "With a new undertaking, there is a certain amount of apprehension derived from the fear of the unknown." He suggested that students may benefit from an alternate route, by becoming a teacher assistant as part of the final training preparation to become a teacher, that would be considered the entry level into the teaching profession. Some may see this as an excellent alternative to teacher preparation, especially because it would provide an extended period of time in the field, working so close to a certified professional. In recalling his recent university course work, Jeff concludes, "The classes emphasizing student activities and those involving practicum experiences will prove to be the most helpful in the field."

The practicing student teacher, Brittany Whitson, is currently student teaching in a third-grade classroom after completing her first student teaching experience in kindergarten. Brittany is graduating with an Elementary Education degree in May, 1994, and has been nominated for Student Teacher of the Year. Brittany describes her first day of student teaching as very exciting. "At first, I think the kids were as nervous as I was," Brittany added. When asked about her most valuable piece of information gained from her student teaching experience thus far, she said it was advice on handling discipline. Discipline procedures can be explained theoretically over and over, and advice can be suggested on how to handle classroom management positively and effectively, but only by managing a classroom full of eager bodies, especially 5-year-olds, can one fully understand how important discipline in a classroom is. Brittany added that even in a good school, with an exemplary classroom full of well-behaved students, there will always be children who require special management techniques to keep the behavior acceptable in the class. Another area Brittany touched on was the amount of required paperwork. Although many student teachers find the abundance of paperwork excessive and an overload, Brittany considered it sufficient and helpful. The paperwork kept her organized and on top of the things happening in her classroom. For example, the daily journal required of student teachers allowed Brittany to have a written history of the events of each day. This becomes an excellent resource for a first-year teacher. For the student teacher waiting to begin student teaching, Brittany suggests that, before beginning student teaching, he or she gather as much information as possible about the age level of the children he or she will teach and examine what the students are learning and how they behave at that level. "A simple background check of third graders helped me tremendously," added Brittany. "One thing a student teacher always needs is to be missed when she leaves," Brittany said. "Then you know you've made a difference."

The mature student teacher is Natalie Breland, a graduate of The University of Southern Mississippi who is certified in Spanish and social studies. Upon completing her field experience and academic courses in December, 1993, she began to search for employment. With her student teaching experience recently completed, Natalie was able to reflect upon many factors that contributed to her success as well as areas where she needed some improvement. Natalie suggested that one beneficial change in the preparation program would be to have university supervisors who had taught her methods courses to still work with her as mentors throughout the student teaching experience. In other words, Natalie states, "Allow the professors who taught me how to teach to evaluate me in my student teaching experience." Lanier and Little (1993) also claim that the value of student teaching is dependent on the prospective teacher being prepared to learn from it. Natalie recalled a friend who took an alternate route to certification by evading the field experience, and told of the ease and confidence her friend lacked in migrating into the professional workforce. An abundance of confidence is gained in making the transition from the first student teaching experience to the second. "Just the experience," Natalie explains, "the more I did it [taught], the better I felt." One issue that many student teachers face is that of classroom management. "Discipline was difficult, because you [the student teacher] are the second in command," she noted. "The second experience was better because I was able to have my own rules," Natalie added. As Natalie begins her first teaching job, she is able to look back at the excessive paperwork, experience in planning three different preparations, and conferencing with coordinating teachers and university supervisors, and feel adequately prepared.

Finally, as the practicing professional, I offer my account of student teaching subsequent to the completion of my first year of actual professional employment. As I recall my preservice training, I can remember my first day, the anticipation, anxiety, excitement, apprehension, and the feeling of success in knowing I had finally progressed to this point in my career. It gave me a sense of pride. After that first week, I realized the importance of my field experiences and the abundance of knowledge I gained as I observed, participated, and taught lessons that I had personally planned. The student teachers who truly have the desire to teach children to love learning will be the talented teachers who survive and succeed. Field experiences allowed me to be the teacher under the protective guidance of two mentors. Although classroom management, the paperwork load, and fitting in with existing faculty may be difficult, the experience and practice are priceless. Now that I have 1 year of teaching junior high behind me and the completion of my master's degree only a few days away, I can appreciate the art of the field experiences, and the initiative I was given to want to learn more, as confirmation of why I chose to be a teacher, my caring about children, and the desire to share the excitement of learning with them.

The greatest benefit I obtained from my student teaching was the suitcase of knowledge filled to capacity as I conceptualized the knowledge gained in my college courses with the practical experiences gained during student teaching. Knowledge, education, and experience, once gained, can never be taken away. Mentors can provide an open-ended guidance that allows the student to blossom into a teacher. The job of the cooperating teacher and the university supervisor is a difficult one. One must consider at the beginning of the student teaching period that the student teacher is a very impressionable, receptive ball of clay ready to be molded into a beautiful sculpture of an educator. By examining this analogy, the fragile nature of the roles of cooperating teacher and university supervisor are better understood. University personnel need to be careful that the seminars and advice during the field experience of a student do not concentrate on acquiescence or conformity with the existing school routines or the mastery of stagnant techniques; instead, they must encourage careful examination of experience (Lanier & Little, 1993). There is always a possibility that student teachers tend to focus on more of what the cooperating teacher is doing, and how he or she deals with the students in the classroom, than on practicing being teachers themselves (Lutrell, 1981). Both the cooperating teacher and the university supervisor serve as guides, coaches, counselors, trainers, instructors, and tutors, thereby serving as mentors. Their job requirements extend much further than those of an evaluator.

In the student's experience in preservice training, peers and other faculty members at the cooperating schools are also important. Peers provide the openness of intellectual conversation and an opportunity for true reflection of the experience. Other faculty members serve to make the newcomer feel welcome and like a professional, which contributes to the self-esteem of the student teacher. Just as Brittany, the practitioner student teacher commented, "Nothing feels better than to hear an outside teacher make the comment on how great it is to see me have my own classroom right beside her."

One aspect of field experience that many people forget to mention is the personal adjustments required. After 3 years of class meetings, with breaks between classes, long lunch hours, naps, social events at night, and relaxing weekends, the time schedule for the student teacher takes a 180-degree turn. For many students it is an adjustment to be surrounded by bright, and not so bright, eager faces that require them to be prepared for 6 full, busy hours a day. As many teachers know and student teachers learn, teaching does not end at 3:30 p.m. or 4:00 p.m. There are lessons to plan, papers to grade, classrooms to prepare, and students constantly on your mind. A teacher who loves his or her work has 24-hour, 7-day-a-week employment.

Upon completion of the field experience program, student teachers should have come into contact with many new ideas, approaches, techniques, and, best of all, experiences. Most every student teacher who has successfully completed his or her preservice training is ready to enter the professional status as a professional educator. Field experiences give students a great deal of self-confidence coupled with enthusiasm. School districts need and want a self-confident, flexible, enthusiastic learner. Field experiences should begin early in a student's academic path. Denton (1982) states that those who have participated in an early field experience can have the opportunity to examine the dynamics of a classroom from the perspective of a teacher early in their teacher preparation program.

Achieving professional status begins with the interview process and ends, the candidate hopes, with employment. In my
experience with this process, I found it best to be yourself and
relax. After all, I am not the only one being interviewed. It is also
important to interview the school or school district for your own
professional insight. Be curious and do not be afraid to ask questions. If one has successfully completed a degree in education,
then one is prepared for employment. The first day in the classroom will be a new experience, but a rewarding one. Every day I
learned something new. University course work aided me in becoming a successful teacher, but field experience made me an
experienced teacher.

Another important element to remember, as an ever-evolving
professional, is that education should always be a continual learning experience. Teachers are extraordinary people who should
always be learning from new experiences and trying new ways to
utilize old information. No one is ever too old, too experienced, or
too educated to learn something new. Education is an honored
profession that can provide the passion for learning as a gift to
anyone with the desire to receive it.

References

Bowyer, C. H., & Van Dyke, J. (1986). *An analysis of contemporary
trends in practical preparation experiences in teacher education*
(ERIC Document Reproduction Service No. ED 286 874).

Denton, J. J. (1982). Early field experience influence on performance in subsequent coursework. *Journal of Teacher Education,
33*, 19-23.

Lanier, J. E., & Little, J. W. (1993). *Research on teacher education*. East
Lansing: Michigan State University, National Institute of Education.

Lutrell, H. D. (1981). *Early elementary field-based experience: A university and public school approach* (ERIC Document Reproduction Service No. ED 212 376).

❖ 6 ❖

Managing Someone Else's Classroom During Student Teaching

ROBERT E. KNAUB

Student discipline has been a concern of parents, teachers, school administrators, and legislators since the early 1960s. To quantify the level of concern, a major national education association, Phi Delta Kappa, commissioned the Gallup Organization to identify critical issues and develop a survey instrument that targeted parents who had children in the public schools, parents who had children in private schools, and other single persons and nonparents. Conducted since 1968, the national survey has focused on a variety of categorical issues. Consistently, school discipline has been rated among the top three concerns since the beginning of the survey. With an ever-increasing incidence of juveniles being involved in major criminal activities, such as drug dealing, murders, and rapes, it is not surprising that parents are increasingly concerned about the safety of their children in school.

Because parents have a high level of concern about safety and disciplinary issues in schools, the preparation of competent teachers who have the knowledge, skill, and experiential background in instruction and classroom management must be one of the most important goals of colleges of education. Presently, the literature indicates that a dichotomy exists between the perception of student teachers compared with beginning teachers as to the importance of classroom management. For instance, in one study the results indicated that student teachers may not be as anxious about their ability to manage classroom situations and seemed to be far more concerned about the academic and emotional growth of their students (Silvernail & Costello, 1983). In another study student teachers were found to be extremely optimistic about their ability to maintain discipline and to respond effectively to misbehavior. Indeed, the data suggested that student teachers were "unrealistically optimistic" about their future performance as teachers (Weinstein, 1988). Conversely, educational research has consistently indicated that beginning teachers perceive discipline to be their most serious problem (Veenman, 1984). This dichotomy of perceptions may very well tell us that student teachers need to have more realistic experiences during their student teaching days in order to be ready for the rigors of the first year. Ralph Tyler, past dean of the College of Social Sciences at the University of Chicago and creator of the National Academy of Education, has related: "Teachers need to understand that people everywhere have certain basic needs for life and learning and that classroom management means capitalizing on meeting those needs. Teacher education is not bestowed by faculty lectures but occurs through participating in active dialogue and dealing with real problems. Student teachers should be involved in solving classroom problems and then reflecting on the meaning of those problems" (Hiatt, 1994).

Because of concern about the preparation of student teachers for classroom management, selected interviews were conducted with 25 elementary and secondary teachers. The focus of the interviews was their classroom management philosophy and how they involved student teachers in management activities. Thirteen of the teachers were from elementary schools and 12 from secondary schools. Teachers were selected for having sponsored at least three student teachers and had to be considered by university supervisors as excellent cooperating teachers. The interviews were held during the months of January and February, 1994. The content of the interviews suggested that cooperating teachers allow student teachers little flexibility in determining classroom management policies, procedures, and activities while they student teach. As a former school principal, I was struck with this inflexibility concerning classroom management. When I was a principal my staff and I had assisted in the preparation of more than 200 student teachers during a 20-year period. I was strongly committed to providing future teachers with professional experiences and encouraged a similar attitude among faculty members. The attitudes expressed during the interviews were a deviation from my own experiences and made me question whether a different approach could be taken to create more flexible environments for student teachers.

The attitudes expressed by cooperating teachers during the interviews echo this inflexibility about classroom management. For example, an elementary teacher in a rural setting stated, "I am well aware of the expectations of this community. When I work with student teachers it is my job to communicate those expectations. I have developed a classroom management plan. I expect the student teacher to learn it and carry it out." A teacher in a larger suburban setting commented, "The parents in this district have very high expectations. They don't want me experimenting with their kids. I follow the established curriculum, set my classroom rules, and expect the student teacher to learn the system and demonstrate that they can do it." A principal in a large urban setting responded, "There are school rules and I expect all teachers to follow them. We have gangs in our community and there are certain things which are prohibited. Teachers can have their own class rules, but I need to approve them." There were five secondary teachers who provided some flexibility for their student teachers. Among these the student teachers were expected to follow the class rules, but they could work with an individual student and attempt to help the student either to conform to class rules or to complete the class assignments. Two secondary teachers indicated (with great frustration), "Do whatever works."

From the interviews it would appear that during the first 2 weeks of the clinical experience the cooperating teacher explains the classroom management plan to the student teacher but generally does not involve him or her in any management activities. The student observes how the cooperating teacher implements this plan and the teacher informs the student that he or she will be encouraged to implement similar management strategies when assuming instructional responsibilities later in the semester. In the initial phase, most student teachers observe several different teachers' classes and, after their classroom observations, are asked to critique the differences among teachers in planning, teaching, and management styles. Many of the elementary cooperating teachers indicated that they hold a debriefing session daily with the student teachers. Two elementary teachers indicated that debriefings were important because they could do some initial assessment about the student teacher's knowledge and skill level of classroom management. The cooperating teacher would then use this information as a base to discuss and plan for future teaching activities with student teachers.

When the student teachers assume teaching responsibilities, usually one or two periods a day, they are also expected to implement classroom management plans. If a student teacher has difficulty with individual students, he or she is expected to implement the management plan to solve the problem. If the student teacher has ongoing problems with an individual student, the cooperating teacher will visit with the student teacher, suggest probable solutions, and expect the student teacher to implement appropriate behavioral strategies. If the problem continues, the cooperating teacher will intervene and solve the problem as unobtrusively as possible.

As the student teachers assume responsibility for the entire class(es), they become increasingly involved in management activities, implementing the plan devised by the cooperating teacher. It is at this phase that most cooperating teachers become heavily involved with student teachers as they plan, deliver instruction, motivate, and discipline students who are disruptive in class. Student teachers are expected to be creative within the parameters developed by the cooperating teacher. One teacher stated, "I have to be sure that this student is competent when they teach next year. I am giving them my model for good instruction [classroom management]. I don't have time to experiment with other models." Conversely, secondary teachers were more flexible in their approach and gave student teachers more leeway in planning. A secondary teacher said, "He has to learn how to fly. If I monitor him too closely he won't have the opportunity to make many mistakes. He will learn from his mistakes." Another secondary teacher stated, "I look at her plans and if they are reasonable, I'll let her try them. If she falls on her face, I'll pick her up and we go on."

Students who graduate from teacher preparation programs exit with varying degrees of skill, experiences, and competencies. Most students have been introduced to the need for effective management skills, but with little opportunity to practice them. Many students have observed videotapes of exemplary practices and receive instruction as how to incorporate management activities during their methods classes. Thus, it would appear that student teachers exit the program with some theory and little practical application of exemplary classroom management principles and practices. If students are expected to leave the university with competence in classroom management, the main body of their classroom management experience has to be completed during student teaching. If teachers provide little room for experimentation during the student teaching phase, how is it possible for these students to gain competency in classroom management? Furthermore, if they are introduced to the practice of only one form of classroom management, they will be ill prepared to deal with the complicated and ever-changing classroom in the public schools.

How can we assure the public that teachers we produce are competent to educate their kids? The answer to this question is multifaceted. First, it is imperative that teacher preparation programs form partnerships with the public schools. In many cases the reason for these collaborative efforts is to share ideas, resources, and expertise about how to improve education, not only for student teachers but also for cooperating teachers and students. If more competent teachers are to be prepared, more direct experiences for student teachers must be provided. The public schools and universities need to collaboratively identify a group of cooperating teachers (master teachers) who can work directly with university professors in developing the theory and practical experiences needed for each student teacher. If we expect students to become competent in classroom management activities, this type of collaboration is a necessity. As a middle-level teacher observed, "I have learned a lot about teaching during the last 8 years. I would like to share my teaching strategies and discipline plans with student teachers, but no one asks me." An elementary teacher echoes, "The university misses the boat in not asking teachers to help with methods classes." Clearly, the successful practitioner would enhance student preparation.

If student teachers are to acquire competencies in classroom management skills, a key person is the master teacher. For definition purposes master teachers are those considered among the best in their respective fields. They have been selected through a collaborative process between the public schools and the university. Basically, these are individuals who invest their talents and time in improving the profession of teaching. Master teachers who are utilized appropriately are assigned the rank of adjunct professor in teacher training institutions. They are then instructional partners with university professors, each playing a critical role in the preparation of future teachers. The professors provide the theoretical base for each of the areas explored by the student teachers, and the master teacher demonstrates the practical application of the theories. Additionally, the master teacher not only has access to the public schools but is also a teacher in the public schools. This access is important for three reasons: First, the master teacher can help with the selection of competent teachers, who in turn will work with students during their clinical experiences. Second, the master teacher can assess the progress of each student teacher and decide which interventions are needed to improve the students' performance. Third, and perhaps most important, is the feedback provided to the university supervisor. If the master teachers identify patterns of weakness in student teachers, this information needs to be considered for future curriculum and program changes. For example, if students have deficits in classroom management theory, course adjustments can be considered annually as faculties review and adapt their curriculum.

Master teachers are central to the student teachers' acquiring knowledge through exemplary teaching, but the importance of the university professors must not be overlooked. These professors are essential to the students' preparation, and many are on the cutting edge of recent research findings in their respective fields. This, as well as new information, needs to be extended to master teachers so it can be incorporated into practical application and reinforced with student teachers through new experiences. For example, the area of classroom management has been identified by teachers and student teachers alike as a critical area. As was illustrated earlier and described in this chapter, teachers have difficulty letting students experiment with classroom management strategies during their clinical experiences. It is of crucial importance that university programs play a proactive role in the training and retraining of teachers/master teachers.

I offer the following crucial elements as components of a teacher education program that produces professionals who have excellent management skills.

- It is important that students teachers have one-on-one tutoring experiences with pupils. One of the more important lessons a student learns is the importance of personal attention and how it enhances a pupil's self-discipline. Pupils who have developed a personal relationship with a teacher tend to work harder and cause fewer problems in the classroom. If student teachers understand this linkage because they have experienced it, they will have learned one of the essential building blocks for maintaining good classroom discipline.
- Student teachers need to become competent in working with pupils in groups. Schools are very competitive environments, and pupils receive very little skill development in working with one another in groups. We need to take advantage of pupils helping pupils. Much of the frustration and acting-out behavior in schools is due to pupils not

being able to learn. A teacher who has mastered cooperative learning skills can enhance pupils' learning and behavior.

- Seminars developed and delivered throughout the semester for student teachers have great importance. Student teachers need the opportunity to share their classroom management dilemmas with supervisors and other students. In many cases other student teachers are experiencing the same problems. By utilizing group discussions, videotaped scenarios, and individual counseling sessions, supervisors can help student teachers think reflectively and solve their own problems.

- The use of reflective journals may be a very helpful tool for the student teachers, not only to recall what they have observed but later to give them an opportunity to analyze disciplinary and instructional situations. The supervisors can read the journals and make note of the students' progress, concerns, and problems. The reflective journals can be a good counseling tool for the supervisors.

- The student teachers will take a series of education and methods courses during their college career. One of the universities' primary goals has to be to develop students who are constantly learning from their experiences, both inside and outside the classroom. In other words, we need to produce reflective thinkers. What does this term mean? Reflective thinkers are those who are constantly learning from what they experience both inside and outside the classroom. They find new ways to increase their skill and knowledge level. In short, these are the continuous learners.

- The use of portfolios is also very helpful for student teachers so that they can collect and exhibit high-quality work produced during their college years. During the first year of teaching, it is important to be able to draw upon ideas about management strategies, class rules, and experiential episodes during clinical activities.

- One of the more difficult problems to resolve is how we help cooperating teachers/master teachers become more flexible in their approach to classroom management as they work with student teachers. There are no easy answers to this dilemma. Many boards of education are taking a tougher stand on school discipline and are requiring principals to have building discipline codes enforced uniformly by all teachers. In many cases teachers have little flexibility in how they implement the building plan. This is particularly true in urban settings where gang activity has increased and the need for a more uniform response is very important. If colleges/universities are going to have an effect on this dilemma, it seems to me that it has to be done either through a required course, which cooperating teachers take before they work with student teachers, or through ongoing seminars provided to cooperating teachers during the semester. It is during these sessions that we will have to provide disciplinary models grounded in sound theory and practical applications. Cooperating teachers are constantly looking for more effective strategies in dealing with discipline problems. We should have little difficulty in helping them if our models are sound and practical.

It is likely that classroom management will remain high on the list of student teachers' concerns regardless of the universities' efforts. This is due in part to the tremendous publicity currently given to the most bizarre and extreme examples of school disciplinary problems. If we can give student teachers the conceptual framework and the practical tools to be good managers, it should relieve some of the concern. The most important ingredient is for students to gain *quality* practical experience in *quality* school settings with *quality* teachers, because this builds self-confidence. Self-confident teachers are likely to take a reflective approach with classroom management problems.

References

Hiatt, D. B. (1994, June). An interview with Ralph Tyler: No limits to the possibilities. *Phi Delta Kappan, 75*(10), 786-789.

Silvernail, D. L., & Costello, M. H. (1983). The impact of student teaching and internship programs on preservice teachers' pupil control perspectives, anxiety levels, and teaching concerns. *Journal of Teacher Education, 34*(4), 32-36.

Veenman, S. (1984). Perceived problems of beginning teachers. *Review of Educational Research, 54*(2), 143-178.

Weinstein, C. S. (1988). Preservice teachers' expectations about the first year of teaching. *Teaching and Teacher Education, 4*(1), 31-40.

❖ 7 ❖

Can Every Teacher
Be a Successful Mentor?

SHARON O'BRYAN

The answer to the question "Can every teacher be a successful mentor?" is a resounding "No!" Although this answer does not surprise any thinking educator, paradoxically many programs and schools assume any experienced teacher can be a mentor. In fact, I have recently learned of a case in which evidently some think even an inexperienced person can serve in the mentor role: One of last year's student teachers is a first-year teacher now and has been assigned to guide another neophyte. Cases like this speak volumes about the misconception that all it takes to be a mentor is to be a buddy. As a former director of student teaching, I can unequivocally state that I have not met the person who can successfully mentor another while simultaneously learning the job.

Definitions of the Term *Mentor*

Yamamoto (1988) points out in "To See Life Grow: The Meaning of Mentorship" that the true mentorship is hard to find:

> There are, to begin with, not many masters in any field of human endeavor. Of these, only a fraction would qualify as mentors worthy of the name, that is individuals of virtuosity, vision, and wisdom. First, they need to be able to see a person yet to be born in a would-be protege. Further, mentors must anticipate and guide the protege to see what is yet to be seen. And finally, mentors ought to see the world they themselves can only dream through their faith and trust in the guided. No wonder, then, the true mentorship is hard to find.
>
> Unfortunately, nevertheless, mentoring has come to mean in many quarters little more than remedial tutorials for academic deficiency, provisions for therapeutic catharsis, assistance in social networking, coaching for professional skills or apprenticeship for career advancement. In such a context, we must acknowledge that yet another human phenomenon of profundity is being threatened by a misguided attempt at popularization and standardization. (pp. 187-188)

In the meantime, the practice of using mentors in educational settings remains, but the definition holds no consistency between and among settings. Often cited as word-origin history, the term *mentor* dates back to Greek mythology and the story of Odysseus, who left his family for 20 years to fight in the Trojan War. Odysseus entrusted his possessions and his son, Telemachus, to his close friend, Mentor. Mentor was given responsibility for the protection, guidance, and education of Telemachus, which required a major commitment of time and energy on the part of both parties. Mentor taught Telemachus to think and to do things for himself with good judgment.

Successful mentors, like heroes, are hard to find. The purpose of this discourse is (a) to identify the characteristics of a successful mentor and (b) to provide information concerning the training and preparation that should be available to all mentors so that their performance level in that role is optimal. What skills, knowledge, and personal characteristics reside within the successful mentor? How would one design the training and preparation necessary to develop the potentially successful mentor? Interestingly enough, being an excellent teacher does not automatically make the teacher an equally excellent mentor.

The Mentor as Hero

In *The Hero's Journey* (1990), Joseph Campbell talks about the pedagogical function of mythology: "the guiding of individuals in a harmonious way through the inevitable crisis of a lifetime.... Linking the individual to his society so he feels an organic part of it. The individual is carried by the myth in a very deep participatory way into the society and then the society disengages him" (p. 165). If one rereads this passage and substitutes the word *mentor* for *mythology* and *myth*, a wonderful definition exists of the teaching function of the mentor. According to Segal (1987), Campbell believes the hero of a myth does the task for two reasons: "First, he does what no one else will or can do. Second, he does it on behalf of everyone else as well as himself" (p. 4).

The Mentor in Education

In educational circles, the term *mentor* is increasingly employed to identify experienced teachers who are selected to assist beginning teachers in adjusting to their first year(s) of teaching (Howey, 1988). Lowney (1986) found that from 1983 until 1986, 15 states implemented mentor programs to some degree, and legislation for similar programs has been enacted in 7 additional states. In 1987 the Indiana General Assembly passed an omnibus bill that contains 24 initiatives to improve instruction for the state's nearly 1 million students. One of those initiatives, the *Beginning Teacher Internship Program* (Indiana Department of Education, 1993), uses outstanding experienced teachers, who also carry a full-time teaching assignment, to serve as mentors (p. 1). The criteria for selecting mentors are as follows:

1. The mentor *must* consent to the assignment.
2. The mentor *must* be a teacher.
3. The mentor *must* have outstanding teaching skills.
4. The mentor *should* have a least 5 years of teaching experience.
5. The mentor *should* teach at a grade level similar to that of the beginning teacher.
6. The mentor *should* teach a subject similar to that of the beginning teacher.
7. The mentor *should* teach in the same building as the beginning teacher.

If it is not possible to meet all seven criteria, the final decision for matching is left with the superintendent (p. 7).

The mentor will need to be aware of the needs and characteristics of beginning teachers. The mentor may need training in adult learning theory, conferencing skills, observation techniques, and methods for giving constructive advice. The Department of Education will offer training in these skills (p. 9).

Is it possible for every teacher to be a successful mentor? Nathalie Gehrke, in *Toward a Definition of Mentoring*, offers another definition of mentoring by McPartland (1988). Gehrke is uncomfortable with the following definition because it is not a realistic picture of the relationship between a mentor and a protege. McPartland declares: "A mentor acts as a coach, much like in athletics, advising and teaching the political nuts and bolts, giving feedback, and rehearsing strategies. He or she provides you with exposure, visibility, and sponsorship, helping open doors to promotions and seeing that you get assignments that will get you noticed. And mentors take the blame for your mistakes, acting as protectors until you're established enough to shoulder criticism on your own" (pp. 8-11). Does every mentor truly excel, possess, or even believe in the qualities McPartland states?

Drawbacks in Selecting Mentors

Ryan (1986) boldly states, "The only thing worse than having no mentor is having a poor one" (p. 33). Odell (1990) cautions that having a mentor in a business context can have a downside. Complications can arise if a mentor falls out of favor with the organization, if sexual conflicts occur between a mentor and a protege, or if the growth of the protege is limited by the perspective of the mentor (p. 7). Certainly, education is not exempt from these same problems.

Two problems can arise in identifying effective mentors when the responsibility lies with local school district administrators: First, the subjective judgments of some administrators, including principals, may be unreliable, according to Rauth and Bowers (1990). Second, mentor teachers need to be respected as competent professionals and endorsed by their peers (Varah, Theune, & Parker, 1990; Wagner, 1990; Weber, 1990).

Characteristics of a Successful Mentor

According to Odell's collected research (1990), it is desirable to select mentor teachers who are wise, caring, humorous, nurturing, and committed to their profession, and who exhibit confidence, openness, leadership, and empathic concern. The foremost characteristic is to be an excellent teacher. However, Odell agrees that an excellent classroom teacher of children and adolescents is not automatically an excellent mentor teacher. After all, mentor teachers are mentoring other adults (p. 19).

The successful mentor should have at least 3 to 5 years of teaching experience. In addition to extensive teaching experience, Odell (1990) imparts:

A person needs wisdom in order to be desirable as a mentor. The specific wisdom needed by a mentor teacher includes knowledge about the curriculum and content of teaching and about effective instructional strategies, including problem solving and critical thinking.

Not only should the mentor teacher evince competency and wisdom in the practice and theory of teaching, but also the mentor teacher should be able to transmit these through guidance, advice, and support. This requires the mentor teacher to be open and sensitive to the views of the beginning teacher. Mentor teachers who possess skill at reflective listening and effective questioning strategies will accomplish the mentor teacher role with the greatest mutuality. (pp. 19-20)

Training/Preparation for Mentors

Keeping in mind these characteristics, let us revisit Yamamoto's three qualifications of a successful mentor: virtuosity, vision, and wisdom. In my opinion, virtuosity entails ownership of great technical skill. Technical skill consists of the ability to use one's knowledge effectively and readily in execution or performance. Certainly skills can be identified and taught.

Vision, defined as perceptiveness, keen foresight, or the ability to be intuitive, supposedly exists in all to some degree. How much that talent has been brought to the awareness level of individuals is another matter. Some seem to be acutely aware and display an ability to look toward the future. Others have not practiced seeing as if with extra sight and are unaware of what is referred to as the big picture. Exercises in obtaining a different perspective, practicing flexibility, and extending boundaries can bring new vision to even the most myopic person.

Webster's dictionary defines *wisdom* as "good judgment, following the soundest course of action based on knowledge." Although this definition appears to be simple and straightforward, it seems fair to point out that wisdom, along with common sense, is not present in all people, educators being no exception. Trial and error, experience, and learning from one's mistakes appear to be the path to gaining wisdom. Emenhiser (1989, p. 127) turns to adult development theorists, who inform that the classic mentor-protege relationship develops between a person who is in his or her late 20s or early 30s and an older person, at least past age 40 and often in his or her 50s. Levinson, Darraw, Klein, Levinson, and McKee (1978) also hold that an age difference of between 8 and 15 years works best in mentoring. Perhaps it is one generation's knowledge and values, passed to the next generation, that garners experience the label of wisdom.

Mentor selection of professionals who have virtuosity, vision, and wisdom, and are given orientation to their responsibilities along with training/preparation, becomes a significant factor in programs that claim success. Bowers and Eberhart (1988) report that Ohio has a preparation plan based on the inquiry professional model, which is guided by the following cycle:

1. developing a plan of action to improve what is already happening;
2. acting to implement the plan;
3. observing the effects of action in the context in which it occurs; and
4. reflecting on these effects as a basis for further planning and subsequent action through iterations of cycles (p. 229).

Knowledge grounded in research and theory is presented during the planning phase, with multiple opportunities for guided practice, observation, and reflection during the course of the week-long training. The expected outcome is a mentor leader who, as an inquiring professional, is able to systematically facilitate the professional development of inductees (Howey & Zimpher, 1988).

Another successful training program, "A Collaborative Teacher Induction Project for First-Year Teachers," was initiated in Texas by a university, three public schools, and the Texas Education Agency (Huling-Austin & O'Bryan-Garland, 1990). A comprehensive package comprised the training program delivered through this project, involving beginning teachers, mentor teachers, school administrators, project facilitators, and personnel from the institution of higher education, the Southwest Texas Teacher Center, and Region XIII Texas Education Service Center. This program was grounded in research suggesting the knowledge and skill needs of mentor teachers. Training sessions included a wide variety of activities, such as lectures, audiovisual presentations, small-group work, simulations, and panel presentations. A set of training materials (including a trainer's guide, a set of selected background readings, copyrighted handouts, and transparency masters) provided the attendees with the capability to train their own mentors the following year(s).

Topics covered in sessions for mentor teachers included communication and conferencing skills, models of instruction, and adult learning theories, to name a few. Topics covered for first-year teachers included unique characteristics and needs of the school and community; activities related to opening and closing of school; policies and practices related to student assessment; general instructional strategies, content knowledge, and curriculum assistance; communication and conferencing skills; self-evaluation techniques; use of technology; and other topics identified by the local facilitating team.

Important to the Huling-Austin and O'Bryan-Garland model was the support network and dissemination system. Several strategies used included:

1. Support/Sharing Sessions—A working definition of a support/sharing session is time set aside for people in similar jobs or positions to discuss items such as concerns, problems, conflicts, strategies, and positive solutions. They feel free from harmful judgment and receive support from their peers and facilitator about their ability to handle situations.

2. Project Newsletters—An informal newsletter highlighting project activities and participants should be an integral part of this program. *First-Year Teaching Tips . . . A Newsletter for Beginning Teachers* (Huling-Austin & O'Bryan-Garland, 1987a, 1987b, 1988), published every month, served to inform mentors as well as beginning teachers and became a valuable communication tool.

3. Monthly Meetings of Project Staff and District Facilitators— To coordinate the induction project and the related research and evaluation efforts meetings held on a monthly basis are essential.

4. Summer Training Sessions—Three-day training sessions during the summer allow for focused attention, which is difficult to obtain during the regular school year.

5. Training Videotapes—To document the process and to help future training sessions, three training videotapes of approximately 15-20 minutes, dealing with the following topics, give insight to participants: First-year Teachers on "What Is the Most Difficult About the First Year of Teaching?"; Mentor Teachers on "Successful Strategies for Assisting the Beginning Teacher"; and Project Staff on "Building a Teacher Induction Project: What Is Most Important?"

Conclusion

The unique nature of the teaching profession hinders the natural induction process that takes place in many other professions. In most professions, beginners gradually assume job responsibilities over a period of months (or even years) and have ready access to experienced colleagues to help them as problems arise. Because this is not the case in education, beginning teachers frequently resort to learning by trial and error (Lortie, 1975) and developing coping strategies that help them survive in the classroom.

Another more easily observed result of not providing beginning teachers with support during their first year(s) is documented in the attrition rate of beginning teachers. The literature clearly documents that without induction support and assistance, many potentially good teachers become discouraged and abandon their teaching careers (Ryan, Newman, Mager, Applegate, Lasley, Flora, & Johnston, 1980).

Additionally, many beginning teachers experience personal and professional trauma during their first year. They lose self-confidence, experience extreme stress and anxiety, and question their own competence as teachers and as persons (Hawk, 1984; Hidalgo, 1986-87; Huling-Austin & Murphy, 1987; Ryan et al., 1980).

Mentor teachers in an induction program also need support and training. The importance of training mentor teachers arises from the presumption that even excellent veteran classroom teachers have limited experience in working with adults and may not have all of the skills and knowledge necessary to be mentors of beginning teachers. Theis-Sprinthall (Theis-Sprinthall & Sprinthall, 1987) has suggested that well-meaning but poorly trained mentor teachers may pass on the wrong secrets of the trade to beginning teachers.

In summary, compared to one decade ago, there are strong interest and strong activity related to mentor teachers and teacher induction. Furthermore, the increasing body of literature on the topic of mentoring and teacher induction provides the field with a knowledge base for future mentoring programs. British anthropologist Ashley Montague wrote, in *The Cultured Man*: "The deepest sorrow suffered by human beings consists of the difference of what one was capable of becoming and what one has, in fact, become." With forthright, authentic concern and caring, training and preparation can be designed for teachers who have been specially selected, because of their virtuosity, vision, and wisdom, to make a difference in what beginning teachers are capable of becoming. No, not every teacher can be a successful mentor, but watch out for the ones who can; they are brilliant stars.

References

Bowers, G. R., & Eberhart, N. A. (1988). Mentors and the entry year program. *Theory Into Practice*, 27(3), 226-230.

Campbell, J. (1990). *The hero's journey*. San Francisco: Harper.

Emenhiser, D. L. (1989). *Mentor-protege relationships among people in positions of power and influence*. Doctoral dissertation, Indiana University, Bloomington.

Hawk, P. P. (1984). *Making a difference: Reflections and thoughts of first year teachers*. Greenville, NC: East Carolina University Press.

Hidalgo, F. (1986-87). The evolving concerns of first-year junior high school teachers in difficult settings: Three case studies. *Action in Teacher Education*, 8(4), 75-79.

Howey, K. (1988). Mentor-teachers as inquiring professionals. *Theory Into Practice*, 27(3), 209-213.

Howey, K., & Zimpher, N. (1988). Designing programs to enable entry year personnel. In G. R. Bowers & N. A. Eberhart, Mentors and the early year program. *Theory Into Practice*, 27(3), 229.

Huling-Austin, L., & Murphy, S. C. (1987). *Assessing the impact of teacher induction programs: Implications for program development*. Manhattan, KS: National Staff Development Council.

Huling-Austin, L., & O'Bryan-Garland, S. (Eds.). (1987a). *First year teaching tips* (No. 1, August). San Marcos: Southwest Texas State University, LBJ Institute for the Improvement of Teaching and Learning in the School of Education.

Huling-Austin, L., & O'Bryan-Garland, S. (Eds.) (1987b). *First year teaching tips* (No. 2, December). San Marcos: Southwest Texas State University, LBJ Institute for the Improvement of Teaching and Learning in the School of Education.

Huling-Austin, L., & O'Bryan-Garland, S. (Eds.). (1988). *First year teaching tips* (No. 3, May). San Marcos: Southwest Texas State University, LBJ Institute for the Improvement of Teaching and Learning in the School of Education.

Huling-Austin, L., & O'Bryan-Garland, S. (1990). *A collaborative teacher induction program for first-year teachers*. San Marcos: Southwest Texas State University.

Indiana Department of Education. (1993). *Beginning teacher internship program* [Monograph], 1-9.

Levinson, D. J., Darraw, E. B., Klein, M., Levinson, M. H., & McKee, B. (1978). *The seasons of a man's life*. New York: Knopf.

Lortie, D. C. (1975). *School teacher: A sociological study*. Chicago: University of Chicago Press.

Lowney, R. G. (1986). Mentor teachers: The California model. *Fastback, 247*. Bloomington, IN: Phi Delta Kappa Educational Foundation.

McPartland, C. (1988). The myth of the mentor. In N. Gehrke, Toward a definition of mentoring. *Theory Into Practice, 27*(3), 190-194.

Montague, A. (1959). *The cultured man*. New York: Permabooks.

Odell, S. J. (1990). *Mentor teacher programs*. Washington, DC: National Education Association.

Rauth, M., & Bowers, G. R. (1990). Reactions to induction articles. In S. J. Odell (Ed.), *Mentor teacher programs*. Washington, DC: National Education Association.

Ryan, K. (1986). The induction of new teachers. *Fastback, 237*. Bloomington, IN: Phi Delta Kappa Educational Foundation.

Ryan, K., Newman, K., Mager, G., Applegate, J., Lasley, T., Flora, R., & Johnston, J. (1980). *Biting the apple: Accounts of first year teachers*. New York: Longman.

Segal, R. A. (1987). *Joseph Campbell: An introduction*. New York: Garland.

Theis-Sprinthall, L., & Sprinthall, N. A. (1987). Experienced teachers: Agents for revitalization and renewal as mentors and teacher educators. *Journal of Education, 169*(1), 65-79.

Varah, L., Theune, W., & Parker, L. (1990). Beginning teachers: Sink or swim? In S. J. Odell (Ed.), *Mentor teacher programs*. Washington, DC: National Education Association.

Wagner, L. A. (1990). Ambiguities and possibilities in California's mentor teacher program. In S. J. Odell (Ed.), *Mentor teacher programs*. Washington, DC: National Education Association.

Weber, C. E. (1990). Mentoring. In S. J. Odell (Ed.), *Mentor teacher programs*. Washington, DC: National Education Association.

Yamamoto, K. (1988). To see life grow: The meaning of mentorship. *Theory Into Practice, 27*(3), 183-189.

❖ 8 ❖

Rewarding the
Practicing Professional

SANDRA WEISER

Student teaching is the most universal component of the teacher preparation experience. Central to that component is the direct involvement of a practicing professional educator—the classroom teacher. Indeed, researchers in the area of teacher education have cited the cooperating teacher as having the greatest and longest lasting influence on not only the student teaching experience but also the aspiring teacher's growth and development long after the student teaching experience has ended (Balch & Balch, 1988; Funk, Long, Keithley, & Hoffman, 1982). Without a doubt, the stimulating, caring, and supportive cooperating teacher is the catalyst that transforms theory into practice and transforms the youthful energy of student teachers into meaningful instructional practices.

Unfortunately, rarely are cooperating teachers adequately compensated for the vital role they play in teacher preparation. Although many regulations and policies have been legislated pertaining to the qualifications and characteristics needed to be an effective cooperating teacher, very little attention and priority have been given to the reward structure. Increased recognition must be given to the one who provides the majority of the time, attention, and professional support during the final phase of the teacher preparation program.

This chapter will examine not only the profile and selection process of cooperating teachers but also the various reasons why teachers accept student teachers, and it will make recommendations for the future.

Profile of a Cooperating Teacher

In a 1991 report, the American Association of Colleges for Teacher Education (AACTE, 1991), gathered information from 228 cooperating teachers to compile a composite profile of the typical cooperating teacher:

- Is white (96%)
- Is female (75%)
- Is 43 years old
- Has taught for about 16 years
- Has been in the same school for about 12 years
- Holds a master's degree (50%) or a certificate of advanced study or a doctorate (10%)
- Represents all grade levels, with about 60% in the elementary classroom and 40% in secondary schools

If this profile is an indicator of cooperating teachers nationwide, it is evident that they are very experienced, are well educated, and have the potential of serving as an integral part of the teacher preparation program.

State Policies and/or
Regulations for Supervising Teachers

Many states have recognized the role cooperating teachers play in the development of aspiring teachers by legislating requirements governing their selection. The diversity of these requirements speaks more to the lack of unanimity on what characteristics contribute to a cooperating teacher's success than to any body of research on this subject. Whether this diversity stems from lack of educational research in this area, or lack of successful lobbying efforts from schools of education, is a judgment each reader must make. What is apparent, however, is the view that qualifications for cooperating teachers are based more on legislative whim than on research, more on political expediency than on meaningful dialogue between schools of education and state government leaders.

Although diversity of opinion exists concerning the desired characteristics and qualities required of cooperating teachers, there seems to be unanimity concerning the mounting pressures placed on cooperating teachers. Increasingly, cooperating teachers are being held specifically responsible for their students' performances on year-end tests; increasingly the cooperating teacher's own pay and job security are tied to student performance. The thought of turning over students to a novice teacher can strike real concern in the heart of every cooperating teacher. What then motivates the cooperating teachers to risk their career; what motivates them to continue to serve as that most critical component in teacher training? A review of the literature indicates that there are three basic reasons why cooperating teachers continue to accept student teachers: intrinsic rewards, developmental rewards, and tangible rewards.

Intrinsic Rewards

Many of the rewards that accompany the responsibilities of having/working with a student teacher are basically intrinsic in

TABLE 8.1 Selected Sample of State Policies and/or Regulations for the Selection of Cooperating Teachers

---

* Use of NCATE standards
* Teaching certificate/endorsement that is consistent with that being sought by the student teacher
* (Selection based on) training, experience, leadership qualities, and position in the school
* Commitment to or completion of Supervising Teacher Services Program (10 quarter hours or 10 staff development units)
* Demonstrated performance as a superior teacher
* Must be or have once been tenured
* Good performance record, show continued professional growth, and have the temperament, desire, and ability to work with student teachers
* Meet criteria in established rating forms (District of Columbia)
* Willingness to work with school and college officials in planning and implementing the appropriate professional laboratory experiences
* Good working relationships with pupils, community, school and college personnel
* Active member of professional and educational organizations
* Demonstrates that he or she can work as an effective team member
* Demonstrates academic competence and successful teaching techniques
* Master's degree, including 12 semester hours of graduate credit relevant to supervision
* Representative of or approved by the school/department of education of the institution and be certified as a supervisor of student teaching

---

*Institution should ensure that adequate training and assistance are provided.

nature. As Lipsky (1980) observes, in occupations such as teaching, where outcomes are difficult to measure, a person's own definition of what makes work worthwhile is critically important because it influences what is actually done more than the formal goals and organizational policies of the institution. In a profession that lacks substantive career ladders, vertical mobility, or merit pay, the assignment of a student teacher often brings feelings of self-worth, professionalism, and recognition by peers and supervisors as a master teacher, which in themselves are fulfilling for many teachers.

Developmental Rewards

Coupled with the cooperating teacher's intrinsic rewards, developmental rewards can also be a major motivating factor in accepting a student teacher. The opportunity to help a student grow and progress, the role of master/mentor teacher, and the opportunity to analyze one's own beliefs and behaviors are strong incentives to alter one's daily routine. Master teachers seize the opportunity to grow professionally by analyzing what they do when they are putting their professional behaviors on display for someone else. Having a student teacher in the classroom can cause cooperating teachers to become much more reflective upon their teaching behaviors and philosophies. Additionally, the linkage with the university serves as a catalyst for a closer connection with the classroom teacher and the latest research on teaching. These ties with the latest research, university programs, and the cooperating teacher's classroom are critical if we are to:

1. view the cooperating teacher as a primary reinforcement of the student's total teacher preparation program and
2. rid the students of the widely held notion that there is little or no connection between their university program and the world of practice; in essence, that all they learned about teaching was during their student teaching experience.

Tangible Rewards

Although cooperating teachers accept student teachers for many reasons, financial gain is not usually one of them. When questioning 40 secondary school teachers who regularly accept student teachers as to why they assume the additional time and supervision a student teacher requires, Stout (1982) found that 73% said they felt a professional obligation; 50% felt that a student teacher could help them keep abreast of new teaching techniques; and 28% appreciated having a helper to meet student needs. Five percent identified monetary motivation as the rationale for accepting a student teacher.

Monetary rewards for cooperating teachers are pitiful, at best. For example, in the author's state of Colorado, remuneration for cooperating teachers was established by legislation in 1967 ($75 per quarter/semester) and has not changed since. During that same time period, expectations for cooperating teachers (Table 8.1) and time commitments for student teaching (from 8 weeks to 16 weeks) have increased dramatically. A study of the research gathered from other states (AACTE, 1991) reveals that minimal remuneration, high expectations, and doubled time commitments are consistent across the nation. Based on national averages of $112 to cooperating teachers for 12 weeks of student teaching (AACTE, 1991), the average cooperating teachers earn a fee of less than $.25 an hour for their services to student teachers. A question to be answered is whether, based on the present reward system, they will continue to accept all of the responsibilities of a student teacher.

Clearly, the role of the cooperating teachers must be redefined to reflect the critical role they play as the primary instructor during the student teaching experience, and commensurate status and monetary rewards should follow. Schools of education should redouble their efforts to find ways to link the university preparation and the world of practice. By truly including the cooperating teacher into the teacher preparation program (and adequately rewarding him/her for the amount of time spent with a student), all parties will benefit.

"YOU KNOW HAVING A STUDENT TEACHER IS A LOT LIKE
TEACHING YOUR DAUGHTER TO COOK, SOMETIMES
IT'S EASIER TO JUST DO IT YOURSELF!"

Ways to Encourage Intrinsic
and Developmental Rewards

Schools of education can further encourage intrinsic and developmental rewards, reinforce the master teacher status, and recognize the importance of the cooperating teacher's role if they:

1. establish a set of proficiencies and criteria for cooperating teachers (see Table 8.1) and award clinical or adjunct pro-

fessor title to cooperating teachers who successfully meet the standards;

2. establish recognition certificates or plaques to be presented at building staff meetings by a university representative (usually the student's university consultant);
3. distribute letters of appreciation from the director of field experience or the dean of the college of education;
4. invite cooperating teachers to speak at preservice methods classes;
5. videotape the cooperating teacher or bring a methods class to the school to observe the cooperating teacher presenting a demonstration lesson;
6. invite the cooperating teacher to participate in university/school partnership meetings or university advisory boards;
7. create a newsletter for cooperating teachers; and
8. recognize cooperating teachers in university publications.

Ways to Compensate Cooperating Teachers

- Increased monetary rewards (presently range nationally from none to $500, with an average amount of $112)
- Tuition waivers (presently range from one credit hour to a dollar value of $624 with an average of 2.5 semester hours)
- Dinners, banquets, luncheons, and receptions
- Awards/plaques/letters for outstanding service
- Access to college/university recreational facilities
- Free or reduced rates to school-sponsored athletic or cultural events
- Discount coupons for use at a local and/or university bookstore
- Free attendance at college/university-sponsored workshops, seminars, or conferences
- Special tours outlining the latest library technology, and a library pass

- A parking pass and a map of the campus
- Professional development seminars that will help the cooperating teachers support the student teachers' development and add to their own knowledge base and skills, that is, portfolio development, supervision skills, and so on

Ways to Train Cooperating
Teachers in Supervisory Techniques

- Biweekly seminars for cooperating teachers (located in several convenient sites)
- Correspondence courses, complete with appropriate technology
- On-campus course work that will be accepted as part of a degree program
- Building-level training done by university supervisors
- Use of interactive technology that would allow direct communication between the university and schools that are hosting student teachers

Successful cooperating teachers have close linkages with teacher preparation programs and have been trained in the supervision process. Unfortunately, resources for supervisory training for cooperating teachers have not been a university priority. As Cornish (1979) noted:

> If one accepts the importance of the cooperating teacher and the university supervisor on the student teacher, then one must be amazed that in our multimillion dollar educational system so little is done to give the proper training to these two key personnel. There is a need for a well organized educational program for those people working with student teachers. (p. 17)

A 1984 survey of member institutions of the American Association of Colleges for Teacher Education found that formal supervisory training was seldom among the criteria for selection of cooperating teachers (Kingen, 1984). Lack of time, training, and experience in supervision can create difficulties for cooperating teachers, difficulties that can often be alleviated by developing supervisory skills. Additionally, research has clearly shown that such training produces change in the behavior of cooperating teachers and has been demonstrated to promote more desirable behavior in student teachers working with trained cooperating teachers (Metcalf & Shillington, 1989). Teacher preparation programs should make every effort to provide supervisory training as part of the cooperating teacher's assignment for a student teacher. Too often university teacher educators lament that cooperating teachers are "just not interested" in student teacher supervisory training. Perhaps these busy teachers are unwilling to assume yet another duty (usually at their own time and expense), and it should be the duty of the university to creatively structure the necessary training.

Summary

In short, cooperating teachers are expected to be skilled in all instructional areas, assume the majority of responsibility for assisting and guiding the student teachers through the essential portion of their teacher preparation, and still, as classroom teachers, retain the ultimate responsibility for the academic success and social well-being of their students.

Currently, it appears that what was once a marriage of mutual respect and mutual benefit between schools of education and cooperating teachers has, unfortunately, turned into a marriage of convenience. Schools of education appear to be taking advantage of and benefiting from the goodwill and professionalism of the cooperating teacher, without an accompanying increase in the benefits accorded to cooperating teachers and the school systems that employ them. A solid marriage requires partners who react to the changing needs and roles of each other. Motivation systems that have changed little in the past 25 years diminish the stature, the self-esteem, of one of the marriage partners: the cooperating

These comments made by a student teacher in evaluating her cooperating teacher support a well-documented finding in the literature on supervision: Cooperating teachers (teachers who serve as classroom supervisors) have a profound influence on their student teachers (Haberman & Harris, 1982; McIntyre, 1984; Zeichner, 1980). Another well-documented finding is that the school experience during student teaching overrides the university experience provided in content and methodology courses when the two are incompatible (Zeichner & Teitelbaum, 1982). For these reasons, and because reform initiatives aimed at improving student learning must include initiatives to improve the way teachers are prepared, the role of student teaching supervisors represents a very important issue for consideration by educators.

The purpose of this chapter is to both examine the critical role of supervision in the professional development of new teachers and discuss the elements needed to prepare supervisors to carry out their responsibilities in an effective manner. A course currently offered at the University of Kentucky is presented as a model for preparing these individuals.

Characteristics of Effective
Student Teaching Supervisors

There is little disagreement about the characteristics effective supervisors should possess. Student teaching program manuals uniformly describe supervisors as professionals who can guide and evaluate student teachers' actions and decisions. Actually, most teacher education programs appoint three supervisors to work with each student teacher: (a) a school-based cooperating teacher who assumes the major responsibility for supervision in the classroom on a daily basis, (b) a university faculty member who serves as facilitator and consultant by making frequent observational visits to the schools and coordinating on-campus seminars, and (c) a school principal who oversees the placement process and orients student teachers to the school environment.

Ideally, this supervisory triad should serve as a catalyst, enabling the candidate to make a successful transition from the role of student to that of full-time teacher. Through their unique and overlapping roles, these supervisors help student teachers develop the knowledge, attitudes, and skills needed to foster learning in their students. For the triad to function effectively, each supervisor is expected to make specific contributions. Cooperating teachers should be able to analyze their teaching practice and help their student teachers do the same. University supervisors should provide a theoretical/research base for teaching practice, evaluate the student teacher's progress at regular intervals, and keep communication among all team members open and constructive. As the instructional leaders of their schools, principals should help student teachers fit into the total school program by creating a positive attitude among staff, students, and parents about the student teacher's role, explaining school policies and procedures to student teachers, and assisting with the evaluation of the student teacher's performance.

As any director of student teaching can attest, however, supervision usually operates under less than ideal circumstances. Because of their demanding schedules, principals often become silent, invisible partners. Burdened with a myriad of campus responsibilities, university faculty frequently do not have sufficient time to fully collaborate with cooperating teachers, and cooperating teachers, in their desire to be nurturing and supportive, frequently do not provide formal specific criticism for the student teacher, particularly if it is negative. In a 1988 study, Richardson-Koehler found that cooperating teachers were unwilling to share negative criticism with their student teachers. For example, in three-way meetings (with cooperating teachers, university supervisors, and student teachers), cooperating teachers tended to defend the student teachers regarding issues about which they had privately expressed concern to the university supervisor beforehand.

It appears, then, that instead of offering a broad spectrum of advice in a complementary manner, the triad can be reduced to a disjointed dyad, with the university and classroom supervisor offering independent and sometimes conflicting advice. At the very least, this diminishes the potential growth opportunities for student teachers. In some cases, this approach even results in poorly prepared teachers who perpetuate the use of ineffective teaching methods.

Defining Specific Standards for Supervision

Although disconcerting, this situation is not impossible to remedy. One possibility is to require supervisors to meet specified standards. Although most state departments of education (SDEs) require cooperating teachers to hold advanced degrees and have several years of teaching experience to supervise student teachers, these requirements do not delineate areas of competence that relate specifically to supervision. In addition, few if any SDEs stipulate qualifications for the principals and university personnel who are involved. Just as there is a widely held misconception that anyone can learn to teach, with little or no preparation, some policymakers erroneously think that supervision merely involves knowing how to teach.

In order for student teachers to develop into the kind of self-directed, analytical, adaptable professionals that are needed to meet the challenges of contemporary schools, they need supervisors who can articulate elements of effective practice and promote growth in others. Clearly defined standards would promote high-quality supervision. Standards should describe effective instructional strategies; knowledge about the teaching/learning process including theories and research findings reported in the professional literature; and skills in problem solving, teacher evaluation, and coaching. They should also address understanding of teacher development and an ability to facilitate development.

In addition to setting standards, consideration should also be given to how those standards are measured. The teacher assessment centers proposed by policymakers in various states offer one vehicle for implementing such a system. However, because these centers have not yet been established, and because they may be rather costly to implement, other approaches must be considered, especially those that can be implemented within already existing structures, such as preparation programs that can be coordinated and monitored at a local level.

Preparing Effective
Student Teaching Supervisors

Preparation programs for supervisors can take on various forms, depending on the situation and the level of experience of those involved. In situations where experienced supervisors are used, for example, preparation may simply amount to communicating expectations and working to maintain a good communication system with members of the supervisory team. Annual or semiannual meetings conducted with supervisors to discuss and evaluate policies, procedures, and concerns would help keep the channels of communication open among team members, clarify roles, and determine commitment. In other cases, workshops or a series of workshops may be required to review current supervisory practices. For example, first-time supervisors can benefit from a sustained course of study in which pertinent issues are examined, skills are developed, and materials are designed for use with student teachers. This is the approach taken to prepare supervisors to work with the student teaching program at the University of Kentucky.

One Model: A Graduate-Level Course of Study

For the past decade, the University of Kentucky has offered a graduate-level course in student teaching supervision for classroom (cooperating) teachers and new university supervisors (both full- and part-time) who work with the teacher education program. Although the course is open to school principals, they do not generally choose to participate. This 16-week, three-credit-hour course is designed to prepare supervisors for their role and train them to work collaboratively with other team members. It also affords the university an opportunity to assess participants' supervisory skills before they work with student teachers.

Course Content

The course is organized into three sections to help participants think about major areas of supervision: analyzing effective teaching practice, evaluating teacher effectiveness, and promoting effectiveness in new teachers. Before introducing these sections, an overview is provided of teacher education in general and the program at the University of Kentucky in particular. For example, because student teachers at this university are required to develop portfolios, the purposes and procedures of portfolios are explained along with other requirements for student teaching. The roles and responsibilities of all three supervisors who compose the supervisory team are defined at this time as well.

In Section I, there is an examination of the issues related to effective teaching practice. This encompasses a variety of issues, including specific instructional strategies, classroom management, and ways to meet individual differences. During this part of the course, participants compare the professional literature with their own views and experiences. Schubert's (1991) theory about "teacher lore" (the ideas teachers develop through experience that guide their work) provides a nice way to help participants think about the value of their own experiences and how those experiences relate to the professional literature. In Section II, participants critique approaches to teacher evaluation and hone their own evaluation skills. They also learn how to use the evaluation instruments that are part of the Kentucky Teacher Internship Program (KTIP) and become certified evaluators for this program. Section III involves an examination and development of the skills necessary for effective coaching; that is, how to assess the student teacher's developmental level and facilitate movement to higher levels through reflective listening and constructive criticism. During this time, participants also discuss how to work with student teachers who do not make satisfactory progress and are in danger of failing. The course ends with a synthesis of material covered, a discussion of policy issues such as how to improve teacher education and enhance collaborative relationships between universities and schools.

Assessing Progress

Throughout the semester, participants continually apply what they learn as they complete a series of performance assessment activities, in which they create material and solve problems related to the topic under consideration during that part of the course. For example, when the professional literature on effective teaching is discussed, participants analyze vignettes of problematic classroom situations and case studies of teachers' actions and decisions over time. Vignettes and cases are drawn from various sources, including publications (e.g., Shulman & Colbert, 1988) and real-life examples written by local teachers as part of a graduate course offered at the university each semester. Videotapes of student teachers enrolled in the program are also used to spark discussion. Participants are expected to generate alternative solutions to these dilemmas, based on the professional literature and their professional expertise. At this time, they also write an essay about classroom management in which they critique the literature and relate it to school and classroom policies.

When they have discussed various techniques for teacher evaluation and have learned how to use the KTIP evaluation system, participants design and/or select a set of evaluation instruments for use with future student teachers, together with a rationale for each instrument in the set. They also develop a supervisor's platform in which they describe their philosophy of education, approach to teaching, and approach to supervision. The idea of the platform is taken from Sergiovanni and Starratt's (1988) description of the educational platform. This exercise is the one participants seem to find most difficult. In particular, they report grappling with the incongruities that exist between what they believe to be desirable practice and what they must do out of necessity. They also find it difficult to explicate and justify their theoretical assumptions.

The final project, which each participant presents to the whole class at the end of the course, involves designing a handbook to use with student teachers. The handbook provides background information and direction for the placement. Included is a statement of the supervisor's philosophy, policies, and practices, which is drawn partially from the supervisor's platform and the classroom management plan developed earlier in the semester. Also included is a plan for working with student teachers, instruments for conducting observations and conferences (also developed during the semester), exercises for student teachers to complete, reference material for their use during the placement period, and school and classroom policies. Most handbooks also offer student teachers "tips for success," and each book contains unique features.

The student teaching exercises often prove to be the most interesting aspect of the handbooks. These suggest a wide range of activities, from short reports about individual students to critiques of the handbook itself. Some pose questions to be answered during the initial days of the placement, to direct attention to certain aspects of classroom life (e.g., What student characteristics do you expect to see at this level, and what evidence do you see of that in this classroom?). Others require student teachers to contribute exercises and/or material that future student teachers might find meaningful.

Assignments are graded and they are tailored to meet individual participants' needs. University supervisors, for example, frequently choose to design a syllabus and seminar program for the student teaching course in place of the handbook, which is more suited to cooperating teachers. Some supervisors even design a plan for professional development workshops and/or a syllabus for a supervision course.

Course Evaluations

Course evaluations consistently indicate that participants find the course useful. Some participants comment that they have sharpened their own teaching skills and deepened the way they think about their teaching/learning process. Many report that they are pleased to be certified evaluators for the Kentucky Teacher Internship Program because it affords them the opportunity to guide and assist first-year teachers. Most who question the value of writing the supervisor's platform during the semester admit, at the end of the semester, that the exercise helped them examine their assumptions about teaching and organize the insights gained from experience into concrete form.

In addition to the course evaluations, the student teachers' evaluations of those who have taken the course serve as another indicator of its effectiveness. Participants who serve as supervisors generally receive high ratings for their supervisory skills.

Ensuring Effective Supervision

The University of Kentucky course has proven to be a valuable endeavor for several reasons. It helps participants relate scholarly theories and research findings to their own experiences as educators in a practical way, it helps the university maintain a qualified supervisory staff, and it helps cooperating teachers and university supervisors forge meaningful partnerships. It has proven to be an especially effective vehicle for preparing part-time university supervisors and acquainting them with our program. However, it does not address the need for including the principal as an integral team member, nor does it ensure that what is learned during the course will be implemented on a long-term basis. Supervisors are busy professionals who are expected to play multiple roles, the least recognized of which may be working with the student teaching program.

Therefore, it is incumbent upon universities to ensure that all team members are fully apprised of their responsibilities and are willing to take the time to carry them out. Universities must also take the lead in providing regular opportunities for discussion and renewal for all supervisors. Involving cooperating teachers and school principals in seminars and meetings to discuss supervisory issues can facilitate that. Frequent meetings and collaborative projects will also create opportunities for supervisors to discuss problematic cases and explore ways to avoid failure of student teachers.

The success of the Kentucky course highlights the value of supervisory training and the need for more consistent attention to the role of supervision in preparing and sustaining an effective teaching force. Supervisors can and do make a difference in the preparation of teachers, and it is important to make sure it is a positive difference. Standards for supervision should be included in the standards for experienced teachers now being considered for adoption by the National Board for Professional Standards and other standard-setting groups. Although supervisors bring a wealth of experience and maturity to the student teaching experience, experience alone is not a sufficient prerequisite for assuming this important role. In order to be qualified to supervise student teachers, educators need to be able to explain how and why certain practices work. This can be achieved through continuous, collaborative efforts aimed at improving teacher preparation and through the enforcement of mandatory standards for supervision.

Note

1. This quotation was taken from a student teacher's evaluation of her cooperating teacher; the teacher's name has been changed to ensure anonymity.

References

Haberman, M., & Harris, P. (1982). State requirements for cooperating teachers. *Journal of Teacher Education, 33*(3), 45-47.

McIntyre, D. J. (1984). A response to the critics of field experience supervision. *Journal of Teacher Education, 35*(3), 42-45.

Richardson-Koehler, V. (1988). Barriers to the effective supervision of student teaching: A field study. *Journal of Teacher Education, 34*(2), 28-34.

Schubert, W. (1991). Teacher lore: A basis for understanding praxis. In C. Witherell & N. Noddings (Eds.), *Stories lives tell* (pp. 207-233). New York: Teachers College Press.

Sergiovanni, T., & Starratt, R. (1988). *Supervision: Human perspectives.* New York: McGraw-Hill.

Shulman, J., & Colbert, J. (Eds.). (1988). *The intern teacher casebook.* San Francisco: Far West Laboratory for Educational Research and Development, ERIC Clearinghouse on Educational Management, and ERIC Clearinghouse on Teacher Education.

Zeichner, K., & Teitelbaum, K. (1982). Personalized and inquiry-oriented teacher education: An analysis of two approaches to the development of curriculum for field-based experiences. *Journal of Education for Teaching, 8*(2), 95-117.

Zeichner, K. M. (1980). Myths and realities: Field-based experiences in preservice teacher education. *Journal of Teacher Education, 31*(6), 45-55.

❖ 10 ❖

Connecting Purposes

Administrators' Views of Field Experiences

GLORIA APPELT SLICK

Many references have been made to the critical nature of the collaborative relationship in teacher preparation programs between teacher preparation field experience programs and the public schools. It is imperative that field experience programs and public schools function in concert so that novice teachers are provided quality field experiences in order to prepare them for the challenges of the profession. In Chapter 2 of his book, *Teachers for Our Nation's Schools*, Goodlad develops 19 postulates that address the conditions necessary for effective teacher education. Postulate 15 states:

> Programs for the education of educators must assure for each candidate the availability of a wide array of laboratory settings for observation, hands-on experiences, and

> exemplary schools for internships and residencies; they
> must admit no more students to their programs than can
> be assured these quality experiences. (Goodlad, 1990, p. 61)

He goes on to say that settings for internships and residencies
must be examples of the best educational practices that schools
and universities are able to develop together and the internships
obviously must be conducted collaboratively (Goodlad, 1990,
p. 61). The success of such a relationship can make or break the
effectiveness of teacher preparation programs. So far, in this book
and the previous two books, the significance of this relationship
has been viewed from the perspective of teacher preparation
programs, and specifically, the field experience office. In this
chapter, however, the public school administrator's perspective of
the significance of field experiences in teacher preparation will be
examined. Of what benefit is it to the public schools and the
administrators running those schools to be involved in teacher
preparation, and specifically the field experience component of it?
Perhaps the answer seems obvious; however, a closer look at the
issues surrounding this unique relationship between the university and the public schools reveals more specific information that
can prove to be helpful to both parties involved.

The Research Design

The purpose of a major research survey, conducted during the
fall semester of 1994, was to determine administrators' views
concerning field experience programs on their campuses. The
survey was sent to 1,500 practicing principals in the 50 states of
the United States of America. This number represented a random
sampling of administrators taken from each state. Principals were
asked to respond to items that generated both quantitative and
qualitative data. The survey questionnaire is included in Table
10.1 at the end of this chapter. The survey solicits information
regarding the placement procedures of university students in
school districts for preservice preparatory experiences. The principals are asked if their teachers receive training or compensation
for working with preservice teachers from the university. Ques-

tions 10 and 11 seek to determine if any school personnel serve in decision-making capacities regarding the procedures and policies of field experience programs at the local universities with whom the school districts work. Most of the rest of the survey asks the principals to identify what they feel to be important aspects of a field experience program as well as their opinion about the expertise of the preservice teachers who have been in their buildings. Almost to a person, the administrators answering this survey felt that field experiences are very important in teacher preparation programs. However, their answers regarding the significance of field experiences to their school district brought a variety of answers from them.

Sampling Demographics

Before proceeding further with the information gleaned from the survey, it is important to have a perspective of the demographic profile of the respondents to the survey. A random sampling of representative administrators was taken from each of the 50 states. To date, 36 of the 50 states are represented in the responses received. The entire survey was sent through bulk mail; therefore, some of the potential respondents have not had time to receive, fill out, and return the survey. The data reported is preliminary, however representative, because the responses are still coming in at this writing. There are some obvious consistent results emerging from this preliminary data. Those administrators responding hold positions as high school principals, middle school principals, and elementary principals. It was important to obtain administrators' perceptions of field experience components in teacher preparation in order to determine the effectiveness of public school/university collaborative endeavors from the practitioners' point of view. What university and college personnel may want, and even anticipate, to be occurring in the field may in fact be something entirely different from what was intended. The largest percentage of the respondents were elementary principals, which stands to reason because there are a larger number of elementary schools than high schools or middle schools in the country. Seventy-six percent of all the principals responding to the

survey were men, and 24% were women. The least number of
women principals occurred at the high school level. The women
principals were at the elementary level, but even there they were
outnumbered two to one by men. Although it was not the intention of this survey to identify gender related to administrative
positions in the profession, it became obvious from this sampling
that, on the whole, administrative responsibilities at the principal
level are still currently dominated by men.

Responses from the northeast came from Pennsylvania, New
York, Maine, Vermont, Massachusetts, Delaware, Connecticut,
New Jersey, and New Hampshire. The southeast was represented
by Virginia, West Virginia, Washington, D.C., North Carolina,
South Carolina, Georgia, and Florida. Responses came from the
southern states of Tennessee, Arkansas, Mississippi, and Louisiana. Midwestern states were represented by Kentucky, Missouri,
Ohio, Illinois, Indiana, Iowa, Michigan, Wisconsin, and Minnesota. Central states was represented by Oklahoma, Nebraska,
Kansas, South Dakota, and North Dakota. Responses have come
from the Southwest, Texas; the West, California; and the North-
west, Montana. All in all, there has been a very positive response
from a very widespread representation of states. The states that
remain to be heard from are principally from the western and
northwestern regions of the country. It is assumed that the lack
of response from this regional area is due to the bulk mailing
process.

The Instrument

The 21-item questionnaire, titled *Administrators' Perceptions of
Clinical Programs in Teacher Preparation*, was developed at The
University of Southern Mississippi by Dr. Gloria Appelt Slick. A
copy of the survey instrument is included in Table 10.1. Some of
the many purposes of the survey were to determine the awareness
level of administrators with regard to the operation, function, and
purpose of field experiences in their schools. Another main purpose was to determine the administrators' view of the real merit
of field experiences, and what they believed to be the critical

aspects of those field experiences. The reporting of the information gained from the survey will be handled item by item and then a summary of the findings will be provided.

Item #1: Does your school work with a college/university's field experience program by having preservice teachers on your campus? All of the respondents to the survey indicated that they were involved, through their district, with collaborative arrangements with local colleges and/or universities in placing preservice teachers in their schools for field experiences.

Item #2: Who from your district makes the arrangements for placing students in field experience programs on your campus? Of the four choices provided by the survey: (a) campus administrator, (b) university director of field experiences, (c) district central office person, and (d) district superintendent, the majority of the respondents indicated that the individual school, campus administrator made the arrangements for placing preservice teachers for field experiences. A district central office person was the next most likely to handle such placements, and occasionally, a university director of field experiences was the person responsible.

Item #3: What kind of field experience programs are on your campus(es)? The two most frequent types of field experiences on the campuses of the respondents to this survey were classroom observation visits by preservice teachers and student teaching involving full-time practice teaching in assigned classrooms at a local school. A small percentage of the respondents indicated that their classrooms were used for preservice teachers to observe small-group instruction and occasionally teach in small groups. This type of observation and teaching usually occurred in conjunction with university methods classes.

Item #4: How are the university/college students assigned to a teacher(s) in your building? Sixty-four percent of the respondents indicated that field experience placements were made by the building principal, who assigned the university students to model teachers. Teachers volunteering and selecting students, as well as central office personnel making the field placement assignments, ran as equal seconds to the principal making the assignments. Less than 1% of the assigned placements were made by field experience directors, as reported by the public school administrators in this survey.

Items #5, 6, and 7. These three items deal with the training of the cooperating teachers to be effective mentors for student teachers. *Item #5: Does your district provide any training for your teachers to work with student teachers or other students participating in field experience programs?* Thirty-one percent of the respondents indicated that their district did not provide teachers any training to work with student teachers. *Item #6: Does the university/college provide teachers in your district with training to become effective mentors for preservice teachers?* Fifty-one percent said "No" and 49% said "Yes." Based on the responses to Item #6, one can surmise that approximately half of the universities/colleges saw a need to prepare cooperating teachers to be trained as mentors, and half saw no need for this. Although this may appear so on the surface, it is quite possible that other factors influenced those who responded in the negative. To provide training for classroom teachers to be effective mentors, there must be time and money available for the training. Another factor critical to the success of mentor training programs is incentive for the practicing teacher to participate in such training. Serving as a mentor or supervisor of a neophyte teacher is time-consuming and adds more responsibility and stress to an already full plate of responsibilities. By adding more training to this seldom rewarded responsibility of supervising a beginning teacher, the possibility of weeding out some potentially good mentors becomes even more of a reality. Those respondents who indicated that the university provided additional training for cooperating teachers shared the variety of ways that the training occurred, in their responses to *Item #7: If the answer to #5 or #6 is "Yes," please briefly describe the type of training.* Some of the most frequent responses were (a) cooperating teachers were given packets of information and an orientation to the procedures for grading, observations, and the evaluation processes;

(b) cooperating teachers were provided staff development by the university; (c) cooperating teachers attended a 3-day seminar conducted by the university; (d) cooperating teachers were required to take a 3-hour credit class on supervision; (e) a 1-day seminar was provided cooperating teachers on how to work with student teachers; and (f) districtwide training was provided. So, preparation of cooperating teachers appears to have ranged from the dissemination of materials and information to semester-long courses of preparation for the responsibilities of working with student teachers in the capacity of mentor.

Item #8: Do you or your teachers receive any compensation for working with students from the local university/college's field experience component in teacher preparation programs? Sixty-nine percent of the respondents indicated that their teachers were compensated for supervising student teachers; 31% indicated that their teachers were not compensated by the university/college for these extra responsibilities. The range of compensation reported in the survey was from $50 to $600. The most frequent amount of money typically given cooperating teachers for supervising student teachers, as reported in this survey, was $100. It is assumed, but it was not specifically reported as such, that the amount awarded cooperating teachers for supervising student teachers was for the supervision of one student teacher for a semester's worth of time. This assumption was made because most of the respondents indicated that the student teaching period lasted for a semester. Principals were not compensated for their contribution to providing student teaching experiences for preservice teachers (except in one reported case, in which principals were paid $100 per student teacher). There were no reported cases in which superintendents were compensated for their part in providing opportunities for student teachers to be supervised in their districts. Sometimes universities/colleges provided other types of rewards, such as tuition waivers after a certain amount of service to the program; recertification points; assigning adjunct faculty status to the cooperating teachers; banquets and staff development opportunities; and opportunities to work with the university faculty in researching state-of-the-art teaching techniques.

Item #9: Does your district reward persons who assist with field experience programs in collaboration with a local university/college? Respondents indicated that their school districts sometimes provided such things as teacher certification points, letters of commendation, recognition on their evaluation reports, and recorded recognition of service in their personnel files. Based on this survey, it appears that rewards for cooperating teachers are reliant upon the local university/college's resources and inclination to demonstrate appreciation for their service to the profession. Occasionally, the local school districts will take it upon themselves to recognize their teachers' contribution to the profession's ongoing development and preparation of new teachers. Consequently, but for the good grace and dedication of caring practicing professionals, universities and colleges would find themselves in quite a dilemma to locate viable and exemplary field experience placements for their preservice teachers.

Item #10: Do you have representatives from your district who serve on advisory committees with university personnel to determine field experience programs' policies and procedures? At first glance, this seems to imply a positive response when one considers the significance of the need for a cooperative collaboration between the university/college institutions and the public school institutions in order to provide preservice teachers with optimum training opportunities. However, this sharing of ideas and people resources runs up against a variety of barriers that exist in both institutions. To bring a collaborative effort or Professional Development School model into the mainstream of a teacher education program involves changing the practices and attitudes of colleagues, many of whom may originally choose not to get involved (Teitel, 1994, p. 246). K-12 teachers may not see work with preservice teachers as part of their job, and some university faculty members are escapees from the classroom who prefer not to spend time in schools, or to do so on their own terms (Teitel, 1994, p. 246). Reward structures often discourage university faculty members from participating in public school collaborative/PDS involvement, because they believe that the university may not value their activities for promotion and tenure evaluations (Teitel, 1994,

p. 247). Interorganizational theorists (Rogers, Whetten, et al., 1982) define partnership activities along a spectrum from *mutual adjustment*, where two or more partners make minor adjustments in their routines and policies to work more effectively with each other, to collaboration, which has a larger agenda of change for each partner (Teitel, 1994, p. 250). Sometimes committees are formed to establish means of communication between the institutions involved in collaborative efforts and/or the development of a PDS. These committees serve as sounding boards and goal-setting entities for the representative institutions involved. It may be the responsibility of the committee to establish the depth of the relationship to be forged between the institutions involved, as well as the process by which the relationship will operate. Therefore, because the field experiences component of teacher preparation necessitates collaborative efforts between institutions of higher education and institutions of public schools, it seemed appropriate to query administrators in the public schools about the existence of advisory committees on which both university and public school people served to establish procedural protocol for field experience programs. Seventy-five percent of the respondents reporting so far indicated that their district did not have representatives serving on an advisory committee with university personnel which established field experience program policies and procedures. Twenty-five percent answered Item #10 affirmatively. This response seems to indicate that approximately three fourths of the collaborations between public schools and universities with regard to field experience programs are operating in partnerships of mutual adjustment. This would hardly appear to be a quality arrangement for professional training.

Item #11: Does your district require a screening process of students before accepting them for student teaching? The survey respondents were fairly evenly split. Fifty-five percent indicated "No," and 45% indicated "Yes." When asked what kind of screening was done, the overwhelming response was one-on-one interviews, mainly with the principal of the school considering the placement of the student teacher. Other types of interviews involved committees of teachers, one-on-one interviews with potential cooperating teachers, and interviewing with the superintendent of the school district. Other screenings included fingerprint checks and review of academic background.

The next portion of the survey focuses on the evaluation of the effectiveness of field experience programs. Respondents considered the benefits of participating in field experience programs with their local universities/colleges, as well as how well prepared preservice teachers are. Finally, they indicated what the responsibilities and status of the cooperating teachers are when they are participating in the local university/college's field experience programs.

Item #12: What are the most critical aspects of an effective field experience program? Of the seven aspects from which the respondents could choose, more indicated that the most significant aspect was (a) well-prepared university students. The second most important aspect, according to the respondents, was (b) teachers who are effective mentors. The third most important aspect chosen was (d) university supervisors who work well with local education agencies; the fourth was (f) high expectations of university students' ability to transfer theory into practice; (g) ongoing feedback and evaluation of students' progress in field experiences was fifth most important; (c) open communication and collaborative planning between school districts and university personnel was sixth, and (e) field experience programs that meet the needs of the local school district(s) was chosen seventh. It is interesting that the second most important aspect of a successful field experience program chosen by administrators was (b) teachers who are effective mentors. Indeed, this is important; however, if we look at their earlier responses to the survey, they indicated that very few, if any, of the cooperating teachers working with students from the universities and colleges had any kind of training to be successful mentors. If effective mentors are so critical to successful field experiences, why aren't there more efforts being made to better prepare cooperating teachers to be more effective? Numerous states have legislated, as well, programs that are to provide mentors for first-year teachers. Most of those states haven't the money to provide the mentors, nor the vehicle for training them. The profession apparently views professional mentors as worthwhile and needed but hasn't quite figured out the best way to provide them and train them.

Item #13: What are the benefits to you and/or your district from your participation in the local university/college's field experience program(s)? The most frequently mentioned benefit to the public schools mentioned by the administrators responding to the survey was (a) preview of potential candidates for teaching positions. Running a close tie for second and third reasons were (b) update of new ideas and teaching strategies and (c) mutual professional collaboration with university colleagues. Under (d) other, respondents mentioned such things as "field representatives learning from practitioners," "another adult in the classroom to whom the children can relate," "someone else who might recognize other learning styles or modalities and strengths of the children," and " . . . [brings about] a higher degree of professionalism in the classroom."

Item #14: In your opinion, what is the single most significant factor about field experience programs that impacts your school/district the most? In answer to this question, administrators frequently reiterated their answer to Item #13 by saying, "the opportunity to preview potential candidates for employment." Put another way, "field experience is a way to determine the successful potential of new teachers." Others indicated that field experiences "help student teachers see reality" and "provide professional experiences with prospective teachers." Another indicated, "we get a preview of what students are being trained to do on the job." Others had a different focus as to the most significant impact of field experience programs at their school or district. Some said that having students on their campus provided opportunities for "updating teachers on new methods and strategies." Still others felt one of the most important impacts was the opportunity for "experienced teachers to work as mentors with student teachers" or, put another way, "effective teachers have the opportunity to serve as mentors/ role models for new teachers." One principal stated it well when he said, "here's an infusion of new ideas and the opportunity for student teachers to try new techniques and learn from master teachers." Many administrators viewed the impact as positive because "new ideas were brought to the school and there was another qualified person to work with the teaching staff." "Sharing of knowledge and lowering the teacher-pupil ratio" were also expressed as a positive impact. One high school principal said, "[Field experiences] are a good preparation for potential teachers." He went on further to state " . . . that my teachers are committed to supporting their own profession [by serving as mentors] . . . " Finally, one administrator indicated, "It keeps us in close contact with updates in education." The only concern expressed in any of the comments was, " . . . there is a lack of teachers accepting student teachers because of the lack of rewards [for working with student teachers] and because [it] requires too much time to work with them." Overall, the responses of the administrators indicated they felt that having field experience programs on their campus was positive, both for the university student and for the teachers and the educational program of the school campus.

Item #15: What kind of field experiences do preservice teachers really need to successfully function as professionals in the classroom? Responses to this question brought out the more philosophic demeanor of the administrators. Yet, their comments were well grounded in the reality of the situation. Some of their comments went so far as to suggest specific articulation of field experiences throughout the teacher preparation program. The following are some of the comments made by the respondents. They also reflect the general tenor of most of the responses made.

"They need field experiences where they can function as a caring, knowing colleague who has gifts to give and things to learn."

" . . . [they need] hands-on planning and actualization of plans and opportunity to dialogue with mentors."

"On-site residency programs that blend theory and practice."

"One-year experience where student teachers work alongside master teachers."

A high school principal indicated that they need "a sampling of all aspects of teaching—experiences with planning, curriculum and instruction, scope and sequence of curriculum, instructional technologies, behavior management, and communication skills."

They need "strong mentors to help with discipline, higher order thinking skills and questioning strategies."

"They need experiences where they are engaged in reflective practices."

"Full-day, long-term (months) situations to get the real feel for what takes place in a building. Provide in-depth experiences."

"Experiences in schools should include brief stints with students as well as student teaching."

"Shadowing experiences should be provided in the junior year of preparation, and before that, guest speakers from the field during the sophomore year."

"Methods classes should be taught by practitioners."

"There should be more interaction in the classrooms in the public schools with professors who understand present-day education."

"Longer classroom experiences that encompass many different classroom settings."

It is obvious from the comments of these administrative practitioners that they value the importance of the field experience components of teacher preparation. If anything, they feel there should be more opportunities for field experiences. Once again, however, they emphasize the need for students to be placed with master teachers or mentors who can serve as proficient and effective role models for the neophyte teacher. Therefore, it seems appropriate to suggest that in order to have an abundance of highly effective mentors/master teachers, the profession needs to reward and prepare our better teachers for such a role. Since it does require a tremendous amount of time to provide neophyte teachers with the guidance and nurturance they require to become successful teachers, it stands to reason that those who do this should be rewarded and appreciated in a special way. Until our profession demonstrates its valuing these people who dedicate their time and efforts to assist new teachers, there will be many teachers who will not choose to participate in the additional responsibility of mentoring neophytes. Conscientious teachers are also sensitive to the fact that the time spent working with a student teacher or beginning teacher is time taken away from their major concern of teaching their children. Yet, a classroom of children in which the mentor can demonstrate teaching practices must exist in order for the situation to be viable for the student teacher or beginning teacher.

The teaching profession must meet this challenge of providing beginners in the profession with the transitional support they need and deserve in order to become more competent practitioners. There is a variety of programs already in place around the country. Some of them have a cadre of master teachers who are assigned to specific schools where beginning teachers reside. They visit those new teachers and assist them as they begin their first year of teaching. Other schools and universities have instructional and classroom exchanges between teachers and professors that allow practitioners to demonstrate teaching strategies on both the university campus and the public school campus. Sometimes professors serve as mentors to students in the field. There is a variety of ways that the transitional stage from student to teacher is being handled, but there are still rough edges that need to be worked out. Perhaps one of the most critical aspects to resolve is just what is a master teacher and what the characteristics are of a good mentor. Remember, being a master teacher does not guarantee that one is a good mentor.

Item #16: What part of your responsibilities with the university/ college field experiences programs causes you the most problems? I felt it was important for field directors and university persons to have a better sense of potential problem areas that exist in our working with the public schools. It was my hope that if we knew of the major problems, we could do something about them. Of the five potential problem areas listed on the survey—placement, communication breakdowns, record keeping/paperwork, supervision of visiting students, and overload of university students on campus and the extra work for my faculty—communication breakdowns appeared to be the most significant problem from the perspective of the administrators. A close second to communication breakdowns was supervision of student teachers. It is possible that both of these problems are due to lack of clear expectations for program operation being communicated by the university program. Sometimes, depending on the structure of protocol between the university and the public schools, the building-level principal is not a part of the regular communication loop. The third area of concern expressed by the responding administrators was with placement problems. Because there was no elaboration concerning the types of placement problems, it is not clear if the problem was with making the placement or after the placement was made. It is important to note that there were just as many respondents who indicated that they did not have any problems with field experience programs as there were those who indicated that field experience placements were the third most common problem with field experiences. Other problems listed by the responding administrators were (a) lack of follow through by supervising professors, (b) difficulty in getting staff to accept student teachers, (c) poor preparation and motivation of student teachers, (d) the departure of student teachers [implying they are missed], and (e) placement of a student teacher who is not ready for the classroom. At the risk of oversimplifying, most of the problems reported by the administrators probably would be resolved if the lines of communication were more efficient and clear as to the expectations and responsibilities of all parties involved.

Item #17: In your opinion, what are the strengths of the university students who are on your campus? The intent of this item was to learn from the perspective of the practicing administrators what they felt were the strengths that university/college students brought with them from their various teacher preparation programs. Of the 11 items requiring prioritization by the respondents, the following were listed as the top 5 strengths of the field experience students on the public school campuses. The number one strength identified was *professional initiative*; second was *rapport with children*; third strength was listed as *organizational skills*; and the fourth strength the administrators chose was *teaching strategies*. The fifth strength was a tie between *lesson planning* and *classroom management*. The other items were on the lower end of strengths and would necessarily be considered weaknesses. The top strengths, professional initiative and rapport with children, might be considered as aspects of the art of teaching as opposed to the science of teaching. The fourth strength listed, organizational skills, begins to reflect some of the science of teaching. Perhaps the natural or art-of-teaching abilities of the students are reflected more as strengths, because the opportunities for the students to develop the science of teaching have at the time of their field experiences been somewhat limited.

Item #18: Conversely, what are the weaknesses of preservice teachers on your campus/in your district? Looking closely at those aspects of teaching that the administrators identified as weaknesses might be helpful in determining what we can do in our teacher preparation programs to better prepare preservice teachers for the rigors of teaching. The weakness of preservice teachers most often mentioned by the respondents of the survey was skill in *classroom management*. The next most frequently mentioned weakness was *questioning strategies*. The third most frequently reported weakness was *assessment techniques of children*. Perhaps, as teacher educators, we wouldn't find the first three weaknesses to be surprising, because they might be reflective of students' limited experience with managing a whole classroom of children. Effective implementation of management strategies, questioning strategies, and assessment of children both formatively and summatively requires extended opportunities to interact with children. Maybe the awareness of weaknesses in the aforementioned areas gives us cause for considering some other protracted field experiences in the classroom for our students prior to student teaching. The fourth most frequently identified area of weakness was *lesson planning*. The noting of this by administrators as a weakness is somewhat disturbing, because most teacher preparation programs put a lot of emphasis on lesson planning skills. Once again, however, it is probably safe to assume that the lesson plan deficiency is not so much knowing what goes into a lesson plan as it is how to plan lessons that fit "real" kids. Finally, the fifth most often mentioned weakness was *reflective analysis of teaching ability*. Emphasis on this skill of reflective practice in teacher training programs is relatively new, but it is something that effective teachers have done for a long time. Because the neophyte teachers are still learning about *how* to teach or implement all those things being talked about in education classes, it is no wonder that their reflective skills about their own teaching practices need refining. Such practices should be encouraged, demonstrated, and nurtured during teacher preparation and subsequently thereafter by administrators at the campus level. In most cases it is the reflective practitioner who remains sensitive to his or her students' needs and who consistently strives to evolve into a more expert teacher, knowledgeable of contemporary practices, available curriculum resources, and ideas as well as technological uses for the classroom.

In reviewing the responses made by the administrators in the survey, it would appear that their view of preservice teachers in their buildings paints a fairly accurate picture of where teacher education students are in their evolution from student to teacher. They appear to have professional initiative and be eager to become a part of the profession; they like children and seem to relate well to them; they also appear to be conscientious organizers; and they have some interesting repertoires of teaching strategies, which they may or may not be able to implement. They are willing, open learners, but still inexperienced, so their ability to work with a full classroom of students and employ all the teaching techniques and knowledge base they have learned about education is limited and still developing.

Item #19: On a scale of 1-10 (10 being highest), how would you rate the importance of field experiences in preparation programs? Ninety percent of the respondents gave the importance of field experience programs a score of 8 or better. Seventy-one percent gave field experiences the highest score of 10. None of the respondents rated field experiences lower than a score of 6, given by only 3%. So essentially, the majority of the respondents (97%) rated the importance of field experience programs in teacher preparation a 7 or better in this survey. From a field director's perspective this is highly encouraging, because we are sensitive to the additional responsibilities required of classroom teachers and administrators who work with the students in our teacher preparation programs. We realize that their plates are already very full and that the dedication they exhibit to the profession by working with preservice teachers is above and beyond their normal professional responsibilities. Therefore, it is very gratifying to receive feedback from public school administrators that indicates they too value highly the field experience process in teacher preparation.

Item #20: What advice would you give universities/colleges about their field experience programs so that they could better meet the needs of your school/district? What follows are comments made by principals as they thought about what programmatic changes could improve and/or augment preservice teachers' field experiences.

"Have more student observation classes before field experiences."

"Get students out earlier, senior year is too late for some."

"Some sophomore experiences would be helpful."

"Have university staff teach in the public schools periodically for a day or more."

"Have college professors and principals work together to develop learning results and/or outcomes for students in field experiences."

"Involve more practitioners in teaching methods classes."

"Form study teams to collaboratively plan with local school districts ways to support each other and support on-site training. The lines of communication must be well established between the university and the school district."

"Establish effective and positive communication with the individual building administrators/teachers prior to field experiences."

"Emphasize the importance of preparation and professionalism. Be sure students approach it as a professional experience."

"Have students well-practiced in the art of multiple/varied teaching strategies. This and classroom management are number one concerns and priorities." A high school principal reiterates this idea by stating, "Be sure students have basic knowledge of instructional techniques and behavior management, and be sure to provide plenty of positive reinforcement to student teachers."

"Don't overload the mentoring teacher."

"Have at least one semester student teaching and 1 year internship."

"Field experiences need to be longer, with a stronger accountability of what is to be achieved."

"Start early in their careers; give them more training in
new trends—more practical experience. Students should
know the current state mandates and also trends in the
teaching area."

"Focus on programs for the urban student."

Within these pieces of advice there are jewels of thought for both
the institutions that work together during field experiences. For
the past decade there has been a great deal of emphasis on professional development schools, and as a profession we have learned
a lot about what works and doesn't work in these collaborations.
What must always be remembered when forming a professional
development school is that such a collaboration requires two
self-sufficient institutions to build a bridge between them that is
supported with common goals. In a recent article, titled "Can
School-University Partnerships Lead to the Simultaneous Renewal
of Schools and Teacher Education?," Teitel identifies six steps that
potential partnerships must go through in order to build a solid
bridge of collaboration. He states that the partners must:

1. Make the decision to collaborate.
2. Establish who will be involved.
3. Identify and select their partners.
4. Define and negotiate the extent of the collaboration.
5. Build inter-organizational structures.
6. Assess and reassess if the partnership is meeting their
   needs. (Teitel, 1994, p. 248)

Although many field experience sites do not approach the
level of involvement of most professional development schools,
the arrangements and commitment are equally important. From
the responses and advice given by the administrators who participated in this survey, it appears that they take the responsibility of
their part in the preparation of new teachers very seriously. In fact,
in the advice recorded above, they mention some of the very
things that Teitel reports in his article. The issues of communica-

tion and commitment, agreed upon goals, and working together for the benefit of both institutions involved are mentioned by the administrators as being critical to successful field experiences. In one of the earlier chapters in this book, the issue of communication is dealt with as a key to the success of field experiences for all parties concerned. In the survey reported in this chapter, when administrators reported some of the problems with field experience programs on their campuses, they mentioned communication breakdown as the most prominent cause of problems. There are many barriers to successful collaborative efforts between these two major institutions, not the least of which are the time and financial commitment necessary to develop a successful program. Consequently, it becomes extremely important for the relationship between the two to be mutually beneficial and to continue to be so. With a common vision and effective communication between the two, this should be possible.

Item #21: What status do your teachers hold within the university community, and what rights, privileges, and responsibilities does it give them? (Check all that apply.) This final item reveals the roles and responsibilities of the teachers who dedicate their time, energies, and expertise to the development of neophyte teachers. The recognition of the role of the teacher in the partnership between the two major institutions is very critical. All persons involved in the partnership are critical; however, the classroom teacher is key to the success of any field experience program. Therefore, the classroom teacher's sense of worth and opportunity to contribute to the decision making regarding the program content and operation would tend to be very significant. The administrators reported that their teachers' status within the university community was viewed principally as a cooperating or supervising teacher (52%) of students at the field site. The next largest percentage of status identified by the administrators for the classroom teachers was that of mentor (29%). A few indicated that their teachers' status was that of clinical instructor (16%). One mentioned that the teachers in his building were designated as "consultants." With regard to the responsibilities of the classroom teachers in field experience programs, the administrators identified two equally significant roles—supervision of students and evaluation of students during field experiences. One might interpret this as the identification of the dual and conflicting role that teachers take on when dealing with preservice teachers, that of both nurturer and evaluator. Principals also identified counseling students during field experiences as a significant responsibility of classroom teachers during field experiences. Counseling would also fall under the nurturing role.

Another chapter in this book deals with the ways universities and colleges might demonstrate their appreciation for the tireless efforts of the dedicated public school persons to aid the neophyte teachers in their assimilation of the culture of teaching. It is critical for institutions of higher learning to be cognizant of the interdependent relationship we have with our public school colleagues and to find appropriate and appreciative ways to recognize and reward those who work with us. Perhaps we should look more closely at the status of the individuals we work with in the public schools and consider elevating their position in the overall scheme of teacher preparation to a level that matches the significance of their contribution. Concurrently, we should reassess the value placed upon a university colleague's involvement in field experience programs. Traditionally, professors' involvement in field experience instruction and supervision has not held much substance in the university's evaluation criteria of teaching, research, and service for purposes of tenure and promotion. With the recent research, led by such renowned educators as Goodlad, Sirotnik, and others, that has validated the significance of field experiences in the overall scheme of teacher preparation, universities and colleges of education have begun to take on a different view of the field experience component of teacher preparation. One can only hope that this view will continue to improve and that, together with our school partners, field experiences will receive its due and rightful place of significance in the total process of teacher preparation. If this survey is any indication of the dedication and concern of public school leaders for the inclusion of significant, well-articulated field experiences as part of the preparation of new teachers, then we have a bright future of collaborative professional endeavors to look forward to.

References

Goodlad, J. I. (1990). *Teachers for our nation's schools.* San Francisco: Jossey-Bass.

Rogers, D., Whetten, D., et al. (1982). *Interorganizational coordination: Theory, research, and implementation.* Ames: Iowa State University Press.

Teitel, L. (1994). Can school-university partnerships lead to the simultaneous renewal of schools and teacher education? *Journal of Teacher Education, 45*(4), 245-252.

TABLE 10.1 Administrators' Perceptions of Clinical Programs in
Teacher Preparation

Demographic Information:
Respondent's Name: _____(Optional) Circle Level: Elem. Middle High Sch. Higher Ed.
School District: _____ School Name: _____
School Address: _____ City: _____ State: _____ ZIP: _____
University/College which places students for field experiences at your school: _____
Phone Number at School: _____

**Circle the appropriate response and/or follow directions specific to the
question. (Use back of page, if needed, to complete answers, but please
number each response you answer on the back.)**

1. Does your school work with a college/university's field experience
   program by having preservice teachers on your campus?
   a. YES   b. NO

2. Who from your district makes the arrangements for placing students in
   field experience programs on your campus?
   a. Campus Administrator   c. District Central Office Person
   b. University Director of   d. District Superintendent
      Field Experiences

3. What kind of field experience programs are on your campus(es)?
   a. Classroom observations—visitations by students
   b. Small-group instruction—strictly for observing interaction in the
      classroom affiliated typically with university/college methods classes
   c. Student teaching—full-time practice teaching in assigned classroom(s)
   d. Lab school—a myriad of interaction situations with a university
   e. Other: _____

4. How are the university/college students assigned to a teacher(s) in your
   building?
   a. Principal makes assignment with model teachers
   b. Teachers volunteer and select student(s)
   c. Central office person matches teachers with student(s)
   d. University director of field experiences selects and matches teachers
      with student(s)
   e. Other: _____

5. Does your district provide any training for your teachers to work with
   student teachers or other students participating in field experience
   programs?
   a. YES   b. NO

6. Does the university/college provide teachers in your district with
   training to become effective mentors for preservice teachers?
   a. YES   b. NO

TABLE 10.1 Continued

7. If the answer to #5 or #6 is "YES," please briefly describe the type of training. _____

8. Do you or your teachers receive any compensation for working with students from the local university/college's field experience component in teacher preparation programs?

Teachers	Principal	Superintendent/District
YES NO	YES NO	YES NO
How much?_____	How much? _____	How much? _____

   Other types of rewards/benefits received: _____

9. Does your district reward persons who assist with field experience programs in collaboration with a local university/college?

   a. YES   b. NO   Types of rewards: _____

10. Do you have representatives from your district who serve on advisory committees with university personnel to determine field experience programs' policies and procedures?

    a. YES   b. NO

11. Does your district require a screening process of students before accepting them for student teaching?

    a. YES   b. NO

    If "YES," describe briefly the process (e.g., one-on-one interviews):

    _____

Evaluation of Effectiveness of Field Experience Programs:

12. What are the most critical aspects of an effective field experience program? (priority #1 being the most important; #8 being the least)

    ___a. Well-prepared university students
    ___b. Teachers who are effective mentors
    ___c. Open communication and collaborative planning between school districts and university personnel
    ___d. University supervisors who work well with local education agencies
    ___e. Field experience programs that meet the needs of the local school district(s)
    ___f. High expectations of university students' ability to transfer theory into practice
    ___g. Ongoing feedback and evaluation of students' progress in field experience
    ___h. Other: _____

(continued)

TABLE 10.1 Continued

13. What are the benefits to you and/or your district from your participation in the local university/college's field experience program(s)?
    a. Preview of potential candidates for teaching positions
    b. Update of new ideas and teaching strategies
    c. Mutual professional collaboration with university colleagues
    d. Other: _____

14. In your opinion, what is the single most significant factor about field experience programs that impacts your school/district the most? (short answer) _____

15. What kind of field experiences do preservice teachers <u>really need</u> to successfully function as professionals in the classroom?

16. What part of your responsibilities with university/college field experience programs causes you the most problems?
    a. Placement
    b. Communication breakdowns
    c. Record keeping/ paperwork
    d. Supervision of visiting students
    e. Overload of university students on campus and the extra work for my faculty
    f. Other: _____

17. In your opinion, what are the strengths of the university students who are on your campus? (prioritize numerically, 1-11)
    ___a. Lesson planning
    ___b. Teaching strategies
    ___c. Organizational skills
    ___d. Assessment techniques of children
    ___e. Reflective analysis of teaching ability
    ___f. Professional initiative
    ___g. Questioning strategies
    ___h. Record keeping
    ___i. Classroom management
    ___j. Rapport with children
    ___k. Interaction with colleagues

18. Conversely, what are the weaknesses of preservice teachers on your campus/in your district? (prioritize)
    ___a. Lesson planning
    ___b. Teaching strategies
    ___c. Organizational skills
    ___d. Assessment techniques of children
    ___e. Reflective analysis of teaching ability
    ___f. Professional initiative
    ___g. Questioning strategies
    ___h. Record keeping
    ___i. Classroom management
    ___j. Rapport with children
    ___k. Interaction with colleagues

19. On a scale of 1-10 (10 being highest), how would you rate the importance of field experiences in preparation programs? _____ Rating

TABLE 10.1 Continued

20. What advice would you give universities/colleges about their field experience programs so that they could better meet the needs of your school/district? _____
   _____

21. What status do your teachers hold within the university community, and what rights, privileges, and responsibilities does it give them? (Check all that apply)

   Responsibilities   *Status*
   ___a. Supervision of students   ___a. Clinical instructor
   ___b. Conduct univ. classes/seminars   ___b. Mentor
   ___c. Counseling students during   ___c. Cooperating/supervising
        field experience   teacher
   ___d. Evaluation of students   ___d. Other _____
        during field experience
   ___e. Other: _____

PLEASE COMPLETE THIS SECTION:

Do we have permission to quote you on any responses? (Check only one.)

   _____ NO, do not quote me on any responses.
   _____ YES, you may quote me on all of my responses.
   _____ YES, but you may only quote me on the following response(s):
   _____

Signed:_____   Print: _____
        (Respondent's Name)   (Respondent's Name)

Bits and Pieces

Everything Else You Wanted to Know About Making Differences for People in Field Experiences

GLORIA APPELT SLICK
KENNETH BURRETT

Making the Difference:
People and Experiences

You can make a difference! At times it might seem that the task of running a field experience program is beyond the ability of mere mortals. It might appear that the myriad complexities of program organization defy analysis. The possibility that happenstance outweighs intention seems probable. You could ask questions about whether the system determines outcomes, or individuals can determine conditions and direction.

130

Yes, you can make a difference! In many ways a field experience program is greatly affected by the quality of individual action; single adjustments in communication patterns, program emphases, or interpersonal styles impact program quality. The wisdom and initiative of one individual can energize an entire program.

You can make a difference by creating a nurturing and supportive environment for those engaged in field experience programs. Students profit from positive supervisory support, clear direction, clear and honest communication, the presence of positive role models, and effective mentoring. Teachers and administrators are encouraged through collaborative partnerships that include specific role expectations, open communication channels, and recognition of contributions. The more closely university faculty are linked with field experience programs, the more consistency can be expected between the goals of teacher education and the student teacher performance. You can influence program structure. You can ensure effective communication. You can pose effective paradigms. You can encourage each member of the field experience program team to contribute fully.

The School Team

Much like the coach on a football team, the field director calls the signals concerning the processes and policies of the field experience programs. The team comprises both university and public school personnel. The success of the field experience programs depends on appropriate team choices and dedicated participation of all those involved. Each person must professionally and effectively follow through with his or her responsibilities, or the total effort of the team will suffer. In teacher preparation, the team scores when a neophyte teacher becomes a competent, confident beginning professional. Working together, university and school district personnel can collaboratively produce a very competent beginning teacher. The team cannot reach its common goal without everyone working together to reach that goal. All persons involved must hold their own so that the results for everyone are the best possible. The school district persons involved include the district central office representative, the school principal, the cooperating teacher, the entire school faculty, and, of course, the students with whom the university student works. The university persons include the field director, respective department chairs, and university supervisors from the various departments engaged in teacher preparation programs. To bring all of these people together with a common goal is no easy task. This is the task of the field director. Much like the coach, the field director must put all the players/persons into motion with a well-thought-out plan for success. There are many things for a field director to consider when strategizing for success in field experiences. The following are of utmost importance. Check to see if you have carefully thought through each of these.

Communication. Of all the matters to be concerned about in running a successful field experience program, communication is probably the make-it-or-break-it factor in every program. A field director must not only communicate well orally and in writing, but the communication must also have a specific and meaningful purpose to the receivers. Frequent communication is also advisable; however, frequency should not override pertinency and relevancy of the communication to the receiver. The field director needs to keep in mind that the persons on his or her team typically wear many hats (have numerous responsibilities) and do not want or need unnecessary correspondence at any time. The following are some suggestions for you to consider in order to provide effective communication:

Keep communication pertinent and relevant to the receiver.

Provide frequent, quality communication that furnishes important information to the receiver.

Provide communication channels through technological advances: E-mail, modem, compressed video.

Provide interactive dialogue by establishing advisory committees as sounding boards and policy development groups.

Provide a program newsletter that shares information about exemplary events and people in the field experience program.

Focus on praising the people who are working in the field experience programs.

Make personal, on-site visits with persons in collaborative districts as well as with university persons engaged in program decision making, operation, and implementation.

Strengthening the School Team Collaboration. Communication is indeed a critical factor in the success of a field experience program. Communication is also critical to creating a strong collaboration with a public school. There are other ways to further strengthen the teaming effort of the public schools with the university. The following are some suggestions for consideration.

Provide public school representatives opportunities to serve on university education councils that determine program policy and philosophy.

Utilize public school teachers as team teachers in university methods classes. List the public school teachers as co-instructors of the classes.

Provide special seminar series for university students that are conducted by public school teachers.

Let the public schools utilize university professors as classroom instructors while their teachers are teaching university methods classes. In other words, let the team teaching collaboration occur both at the university and at the public schools.

Encourage university personnel and public school personnel to engage in research efforts together on a regular basis.

Recognize classroom teachers as professional partners in the business of training new teachers.

Praise classroom teachers for their contributions and dedication to teacher preparation.

Be open constantly to new and innovative ways to involve teachers and administrators in the development and implementation of state-of-the-art field experience programs.

It seems so obvious that the school-university team must be strong and equally committed to teacher preparation. Even so, there are potential obstacles that can blight the success of the team's efforts. To be successful, each member of the team must be respected by the others, and each member must feel that his or her part in the total teacher preparation program, and specifically field experiences, is valued and necessary.

The College and Teacher Education Team

The field experience program is part of the university teacher education program. At times, student teaching is referred to as the capstone experience for teacher education students. Research and folk wisdom indicate that the experiences of teacher candidates in the school setting support their understanding of theory. Many have argued that field experiences in general, and student teaching in particular, have a profound effect on the classroom behaviors of neophyte teachers. Ostensibly, the university community and the field experience program must be inextricably linked.

Often this is no easy task. Departmental structures can fragment faculty. Requirements for faculty, merit pay, and promotion may not recognize the importance of supervision and time spent in field settings. Involvement with schools can be disruptive to faculty schedules. Faculty interest may lie in more reflective activities. Further, for purposes of tenure and promotion, field experience supervision typically does not fall under any of the three categories—teaching, service, research—considered pertinent to procuring either of those much-sought-after professional goals. However, teaching is occurring, though not in a traditional setting, and there certainly is rich fodder for research in field experiences. In general, however, it may be said that the overall structure of colleges does not encourage faculty to seek active involvement in school settings.

From the perspective of theoretical consistency, the field experience program needs faculty commitment and participation. Yet practical considerations militate against consummating this relationship. Herein lies the opportunity for the field director to make a difference.

Practically, what can be done? You may choose to:

Issue a regular newsletter, highlighting students and faculty who participate in the program.

Schedule receptions with faculty and administrators to discuss program issues.

Organize socials around special cultural or athletic events, and provide tickets.

Campaign to secure appropriate salary and promotion recognition for faculty participation in field programs.

Say "thank you" very often.

The area of communication may provide a key to forming this link. Presumably, as interaction increases, so will a sense of belonging. On a basic level, establish a system for regular contact with faculty and administrators, which might include:

A regular schedule of telephone networking

An E-mail network for frequent information sharing

A luncheon colloquium series

A lecture series of guest experts presenting pivotal topics

An agenda spot on departmental faculty meetings

So you have affirmed the faculty and administrators. You have established effective communication channels. What next? Consider programmatic involvement as an option. This is a more complex step. Through this process, field experiences can attain an academic and conceptual unity with the "academic" arena. Some approaches to achieve this consideration might include:

A field experience program council or advisory board composed of faculty who help develop policy guidelines that assist the program director in implementation and leadership

An active teacher education council, including representatives from the university and local school community, to substantively pursue teacher education issues

Through involving and empowering, these quality-circle-type groupings can activate faculty and provide singular forums for addressing issues with multiple roots. Combining multiple perspectives in search of common goals will predictably promote a program unified in purpose and resources, poised to provide quality support for all and positioned to educate teachers prepared to carry forward a tradition of excellence.

Conclusion

Providing the best possible teacher education programs should be a common vision of institutions of higher learning and public school districts. The successful interdependency of these institutions to achieve this vision will determine the outcome of such an important goal. Respectful, appreciative, and professional collaboration between the two institutions will go a long way toward accomplishing that goal. Key to achieving such a lofty goal is open communication built on an equal valuing of each contributing institution. The people within each institution must have a common goal, based on a common philosophy, in order to produce the best possible new teachers. Each institution is only as good as the people who are in it, and when the people there get better, the program gets better. People get better at what they can be when they are respected, appreciated, and given the opportunity to voice their ideas and contribute their talents. Collaboration means valuing each individual's unique contribution to the whole with a focus on what is best for all. It is the awesome responsibility of the field director to tap the many talents of all the persons involved in teacher preparation programs and to bring them together for the benefit of everyone. It is hoped that the questions and suggestions posed herein will give direction for accomplishing such a calling.

Index

CORWIN
PRESS

The Corwin Press Logo—a raven striding across an open book—represents the happy union of courage and learning. We are a professional-level publisher of books and journals for K-12 educators, and we are committed to creating and providing resources that embody these qualities. Corwin's motto is "Success for All Learners."